"In a sense sickness is a place more instructive than a long trip to Europe …"

- Flannery O'Connor

I Will Keep You Alive

A Cardiovascular Romance

by Bob and Adele Levin

Spruce Hill Press
Berkeley, CA

For all people with health issues,
like ours, unlike ours.

May you have the best recovery possible.

May your caretakers and
loved ones have the same.

Bob & Adele

Spruce Hill Press
P.O. Box 9492
Berkeley, CA, 94709

This book is a work of non-fiction. Some names and identifying
details have been changed to protect the privacy of individuals, but
every effort has been taken to ensure that the information herein was
correct as of press time. If you are having a heart attack right now,
please put this book down and call 911. This memoir is not intended
as a substitute for the medical advice of trained physicians.

Cover by François Vigneault
Editation by Milo George

First edition, April 2019

ISBN: 978-0-9972214-2-8

Printed in Montmagny, Québec, Canada by Marquis Livre

www.TheBobLevin.com

Contents

I. AMONG THE LAST GUYS

The morning of January 31, 2011, had been chilly and clear. I had been swimming for five minutes in the smaller of the health club's two outdoor pools when pain rippled in a narrow band across my chest. The pain was not extreme. It did not tingle or radiate down an arm. I did not sweat or sense indigestion. Could be muscular, I thought. You gonna be a wuss and stop or a fool and continue?

Fifteen minutes later – but ten laps early – with the pain unchanged, I called it a day. I showered, dressed, skipped a shave. When Adele came up from her locker room, I said, "We better go to the ER."

Bob is not one to suggest an ER lightly.

I managed an outward calm, until I realized he was losing color. As we walked slowly downhill, I insisted he sit on the bench, which is halfway to the parking lot, while I got the car. The club is attached to a massive, sprawling, near-century-old hotel, The Claremont, which, with its lovely grounds, tall, stately palms, shimmering pools surrounded by blue mats on white chaises, and open to views of San Francisco, the Bay, and Mount Tamalpais, had become our little piece of Hawaii, a year-round vacation without packing and planes.

But alone, as I ran amidst the roses, my terror broke loose. Should I have called for an ambulance? I remembered a few years before, after workouts, Bob had a pain in the chest. We'd discussed going to the ER that day too, but hadn't. Had that been our missed chance to have avoided this? Was I to blame for not insisting?

I started the car, circled back to pick up Bob. We held hands as I drove the short distance to the hospital. It seemed to take forever.

Alta Bates Hospital is five minutes from the club, in a tree-lined, north Berkeley neighborhood of single-family homes. The streets look so placid and the homes so comfortable, it had never occurred to me how frequently they must be rattled by ambulance sirens.

If you want to jump the line in an emergency room, the magic words are "chest pain." But three EKGs, two echo-cardiograms, two blood panels, and the constant monitoring of my heart rate and blood pressure later, the doctors still weren't sure.

After about three hours, the ER doctor called in an on-call cardiologist. Renee Fleur, M.D. (The names of all doctors, nurses – and one or two others – have been changed), a blond woman, in her early forties, was inclined to release me. I was all for that. I was 68. I exercised regularly and ate healthily. I did not smoke. My weight – 182 – combined with my height – six-foot three – made other men in the locker room ask how I stayed so thin. I had annual check-ups. I meditated daily. I was phasing out my law practice, headed toward retirement in the fall, after forty years of representing workers in industrial accident claims, and under less stress than any time in recent memory. My father, himself an attorney, later a trial court judge, and, for decades, a veteran of Philadelphia ward politics, had a quadruple by-pass when he was sixty-one; but he had ulcers and smoked and ate anything and, for exercise, golfed with a cart. As my friend Budd, a pediatrician who'd known me and my family since he and I had been in kindergarten, said, "He did that to himself." If I had any risk factors – besides being male and Jewish – no one had told me. I was a "… last guy in the world you'd think it'd happen to."

But the ER doc was skeptical. The third EKG had been abnormal. The second blood panel had showed an elevated enzyme. And when he had given me nitroglycerine, my pain had vanished.

Dr. Fleur ordered yet another echo-cardiogram, this one to be performed on special equipment by a particular specialist in whom she had confidence.

I watched the echo-cardiogram in 3-D technicolor. (I am not sure I really did, but that is how it seemed.) What had been hazy on earlier screens was now clear. A big wave broke across the screen and broke – and broke – and broke – and froze. Everyone's expression changed. Disaster was about to occur.

When I saw the blood flow in Bob's heart unable to turn the corner, my hands clenched and my feet went cold. Even Dr. Fleur's assurance, "I have never lost a patient in the Cath Lab; a stent will fix the problem" did not stop the fear.

They kicked a fellow off the table in the operating room – the second time he had been bumped that afternoon. Bob's and my customary "Love you"s when parting took on the weight of the moment.

"He'll be fine," Dr. Fleur said. "But we must do it NOW."

Bob and I kissed, and they wheeled him out of the room.

I gathered Bob's clothes from where he had hung them and placed them in a plastic patient bag. He had given me his wedding ring, and I strung that on my necklace and followed the nurse to the waiting room. We came to the Cath Lab first. I wanted to stand by the door or sit on the floor outside, but she said that wasn't allowed. Each step I took away felt more dangerous. At the end of another hallway was an inhospitable room – tiny, cold, and lonely, with plastic chairs that bruised the spine, and an unbearable jackhammering outside the window. Left alone, I wept, then called Marilyn, a friend for over forty years, a UC professor of film. She offered to sit with me. I hoped that would help. I trekked back to the Cath Lab, where I set up camp directly across from the door to wait for her arrival and the conclusion of the operation.

A red light went on over the lab door, and a buzzing emanated from within. I had no idea what either meant. An attendant, wheeling another patient on a gurney, inquired what I was doing there and told me I had to return to the waiting room. I stood, slowly picked up my belongings, and, as soon as he turned the corner, sat back down.

It was the right place to be. Marilyn found me, and that did help. After about forty minutes, we received an update from a doctor who'd come out for a drink of water. (They keep the room warm for the unclothed patient's comfort.) He promised to tell Bob I was outside the door and knew everything was fine. He explained why the red light went on and off. It accompanied part of the procedure and was not the signal of distress that I'd assumed.

My left anterior descending coronary artery (LAD) was completely blocked. My left circumflex (LCA) was ninety percent blocked, but the LAD was the emergency. They fixed it, or I died.

Stents were the answer. Do you know about them? They go into a million Americans a year, but I didn't. Neither did most of my friends. Did they open your chest, one asked. How many stitches did you get, asked another. The answers were "No" and "None."

Not that it was easy.

Dr. Fleur specialized in pediatric surgery, so she had called in Dr. Steven Galloway, a senior member of her group, Bayside Cardiology. He was an amiable fellow whom I had met several years before through another of his patients, Eddie Rieff, a p.i. lawyer and the first of my acquaintances to undergo multiple by-passes. That news had been so stunning I had feared if I shook Eddie's hand too hard, he would crumble. Now here I was dropping into the same boat. I mentioned Eddie anyway. I felt it would not hurt to establish a connection beyond that of body-on-a-slab.

A nurse shaved my pubic hair on both sides, perhaps for symmetry when I was again in locker rooms. I received a local anesthetic. Dr. Galloway made an incision in my right groin. Guided by a fluoroscope, which allowed him to see two-dimensional images inside me, he threaded a tube, a fraction of a millimeter in diameter, upward, through my femoral artery, to the damaged portion of my heart. Through this passageway, he used a wire to break up the blockage and established a blood flow. A liquid-inflated balloon widened it. The clotted material was cleared away. Then the stent, a hollow, metal-mesh tube, was implanted to hold open the previously closed portion of the LAD. (I received two, one in the distal left main portion, one in the mid-left ascending.)

I knew none of this. I felt nothing. I was conscious but had little idea what was taking place. I could hear doctors and nurses and technicians talking, but they spoke mainly numbers. Everyone seemed calm. No alarms rang. No one called for electric paddles. For all I knew, the work was being done by an itsy-bitsy submarine, like the one crewed by Steven Boyd and Raquel Welch in *Fantastic Voyage*. That seemed as believable to me as to what was actually occurring.

The procedure was to have taken forty-five minutes, but I was there over an hour.

A nurse came out when they had finished and said I could come in. Bob's color was back, and when he saw me, he smiled. Marilyn was allowed in for a quick "Hello." I looked around the room, which, with its glassed-in alcove above the operating table, reminded me of a space ship, and thanked the people who had saved my husband's life. One waved and gave me a thumb's up.

I felt elated that the nightmare day was over; a whiff of ordinary life felt wonderful. Bob and I parted again, this time without fear. While they prepared him to be moved to where he would spend the night, I walked Marilyn to the exit, grateful for her love and support. Then I went upstairs to wait for Bob.

The Cath Lab recovery nook housed a honeycomb of curtained rooms that circled a central nurses' station. In our cubicle was a single bed, a large chair in which I'd sleep, a table for food trays, a commode, and elaborate screens monitoring Bob's heart's activity. The staff was relaxed, efficient and kind.

We had arrived too late for Bob to order dinner or for me to get something from the cafeteria, but the nurse brought us each a turkey sandwich, soda and chips from the staff's refrigerator. We were both ravenous, since we hadn't eaten since breakfast. Bob had to keep his left leg still for several hours, so the entry wound wouldn't reopen. Later, when he took his first steps to the commode, he was steady on his feet. I called some family members to tell them where we were. It felt good to be the voice of calm, telling of the harrowing day from the vantage point of crisis-over.

I slept a while, with my head on a pillow on Bob's bed. The night was punctuated with clanging alarms and "Codes" called hospital-wide, reminders that stories did not always end well. I woke a few times with a start, watched Bob breathe, and then, reassured, slept some more. I dreamt I had become trapped on a steep hill that was flooding with water from the top down. I realized my sneakers would be ruined, then my pants. About the time it reached my chest, I knew I was drowning in quicksand and screamed, "Bob!"

In the morning, we moved into a four-patient room on the heart recovery floor.

We read the newspaper, walked the halls, eyeballing the walls, a mixture of paintings, warnings about every aspect of heart disease, and letters of thanks from patients or their families in appreciation of their care. As we walked slowly past open doors, I saw the same theme played out in variations between the sick, their loved ones and caretakers. I did not want to be one of them. I wondered if I would write a note to hang on the wall. It still felt possible to believe we were different, going home, Bob virtually well. Other times I knew we were part of what I saw around us, like it or not.

That afternoon, I lobbied for a private room. I could stay overnight, if we lucked out. I couldn't bear the idea of going home alone. My fear of separation, which I have always linked with disaster, had been fully aroused. Once the euphoric feeling of Bob's having made it through surgery had worn off, I had see-sawed between lower and higher states of anxiety. If we could not get a private room and cot, I planned to sleep in the hallway outside the ward and check on Bob each time I woke.

After supper, approval for a single room came through. The cot, though, had springs that dug into my bones and inspired a nightmare in which the police came to our house and began digging in the basement. They suspected a buried body. When the bones were revealed, I recognized they were my own.

The next morning, I couldn't wait for us to get away. I wanted to walk out the door and forget the last two days. I got the Chronicle for Bob and while he read and waited for breakfast, I stared out the window and thought how much I hated hospitals. When I was eight, my tonsillectomy had been so traumatic that I'd shot a fever so high that my doctor correctly diagnosed it as something that would subside if I went home. He snuck me down a flight of stairs to freedom.

Dr. Galloway came early, with good news – and bad. The discharge papers were ready, but more work on Bob remained. Once the situation had become no longer life-threatening, they had decided they had done all it was safe to do at one time. Bob was to take it easy for a few days, limit his activities to light walks, and see Dr. Fleur to set the date to have his partially blocked LCA stented. As soon as the doctor left, a tech arrived to take still more blood. He said the results had to be reviewed before Bob could be released. I began to fear we would never escape.

After lunch, we were told the results were fine and awaited our turn with the discharge nurse. She arrived with a sheaf of papers for us to sign and others to take home. Then she read to us, for what seemed like hours, a list of precautions we should take and things we should watch for – and worry about – when we got home. By the time she finished, I was terrified of our new reality.

I had already been having a hard time. I had retired, after ten-years as a psychotherapist, to write, but neither of the two books I'd completed had found an agent or publisher. Ongoing, seemingly never-ending repair of our house's dry rot had been depleting our savings, forcing Bob to delay his own retirement, making me feel guilty about my short work history and depressed by my paltry Social Security check. And the fatal diseases, which I had been obsessing about contracting forever, threw me into panic attacks, whether I was on the tennis court, in the grocery store, or waiting for water to boil.

The most terrifying of these had been heart disease. One of my first memories was of my mother's father death from a massive coronary. Her mother had three heart attacks, recovering only from two. And my mother's own congestive heart failure had dominated the last years of her life, which had ended when she was sixty-eight. So I knew hearts. I had tried to control what Bob and I ate and how we behaved in the hopes I could keep us both safe. But earlier that month, I recalled, I had sat, double-parked, while he had carried cartons filled with books into stores to see what they would bring in trade. Now I wondered if that lugging had precipitated his attack.

It seemed I had failed to protect us. I would have to try harder.

II. THIS CLOSE

The first afternoon home, Bob and I went to the French, his favorite cafe, which was on the ground floor of a boutique hotel, in what had formerly been a laundry, a five-minute drive from our house. We took a short, slow walk through North Berkeley's Gourmet Ghetto. We held hands, anxious, amazed babies, discovering ourselves and the world around us. The two days since Monday seemed an inordinately long time.

The first night, unconnected to any machines, unmonitored by any nurses, I was nervous as hell. Any twinge or ache within a foot of my chest's center made me consider popping a nitroglycerine pill, which I had been given in case I needed to jolt blood through my arteries. But my refusals to give in proved appropriate.

The heart attack had shaken me. I was not unfamiliar with death. I had just never felt it applied to me. My sister had died of leukemia when she was five and I was eight. All my aunts and uncles had died. Liver cancer had taken my father. Two childhood friends had committed suicide, one in his thirties with pills, and one his fifties, after opening his veins with a knife. A third had died in a Skid Row hotel of infections secondary to intravenous drug use. But they had been of a different generation. But they had abused themselves. But, I even thought, God preferred me.

My sense of self had been built from doing the same things the same way, day after day, with the same result of another day dawning. I practiced law, representing the injured in workers' compensation claims, which kept me, I thought, on the side of good. I wrote, primarily about underground and alternative cartoonists, which had provided me the material for three books, and, also, authored brief autobiographical essays or reviews on-line. I swam my laps and lifted weights and walked the treadmill. Adele had been the one in our relationship whose worries got us to break routine for home repairs, the purchase of new bedding, or diet adjustments, which I would have ignored. When some new physical discomfort or just-spotted bodily blemish signaled a terminal disease to her, I provided the reassuring calm. But who, I wondered, would believe me now? And who would pay our bills if... There were always "if's, but these were serious and new.

I was unsure who I was or who I could become. I did not know if I could fashion a new, adjusted life before I crashed dead upon some sidewalk. This doubt tested my relationship to others. At first, I only told my closest friends what had happened. I had not grown up during a period when the sharing of feelings demonstrated depth of character. A large portion of me still valued "cool." I did not want to open my vulnerability to discussion. I preferred subjects like what I thought of the Warriors or Thomas Pynchon. When people said, "How are you?", I answered "Fine."

What to tell my mother was a special concern. At ninety-eight, little more than two blue eyes remained to remind me of the woman who had cooked me meals and bought me clothes. Spinal stenosis had chained her to bed in her Center City Philadelphia apartment, requiring her twenty-four-hour care. Parkinson's and mini-strokes had stripped her ability to communicate. Her replies to Adele and my letters had ceased, once her hand-writing had become shaky. For months, if we received a "Hello, how are you?" when we called, we were doing well. We often spoke for minutes to silence, not knowing if she had dropped the phone and forgotten it, or if she had become more interested in untangling its cord than conversation. She spoke in Yiddish, we learned from an attendant, to a blonde girl who lived in her ceiling, more than to either of us. "What does she say?" the attendant had asked. "She wants me to visit," my mother had replied. "But I am not ready." My sister, I knew, had been blonde.

So did we tell my mother what had happened and risk distressing her further than she might already be distressed, if she even felt distress? Or were we to ignore my situation, behave as if things were normal, and risk my falling out of touch with her for several days – or longer – depending on what other events overtook me?

We went for option two – and told my brother Larry, himself a lawyer and writer, who lived just outside Philly, to keep the news from her.

I hoped for a great sleep the first night, but apprehension hit hard, with replays of traumatized feelings. I was terrified Bob would have another attack and fall on his way to or from the bathroom. Each time he got up to urinate, I followed in a daze, knowing if he fell, I wouldn't be able to catch him before he collapsed. I imagined us in a heap on the floor, my already compromised-by-osteoporosis bones broken, or that I would have my own heart attack and be unable to care for him or he for me.

The next morning Bob went to his office. I reminded him that the doctor had said to relax for a few days, but he insisted it would be less stressful to deal with his mail than not. I drove him, picked up groceries and, while putting them away, got a call to come get him. He sounded worn down and discouraged.

It was hard to see him laid low by the burden of work. I wished he would dump his practice, but he wasn't ready. He had conferences scheduled and a trial in April. He decided, though, not to go in again until Tuesday and agreed I'd go with him to monitor when enough was enough. When he expressed disappointment with his current limits, I offered that, after a good night's sleep and a few days off, he'd feel stronger. I hoped I was right.

That evening, we had a good talk. We both felt better, closer and more intimate, knowing that we were grappling together. He promised to tell me if he wasn't feeling well and assured me he could withstand hearing my fears. I knew I'd have to buck up to handle the echo that hearing his fears would intensify inside me. We both acknowledged it would take time for him to restore confidence in his body and for both of us to get over the shock of the ordeal.

My biggest fear came from how close he had been to dying. I could not forget the color picture of his heart attack about to happen, the look on Dr. Fleur's face, and the rush to surgery. She said they would be in time, but I didn't think she knew for sure.

Over the weekend, we took longer and longer walks, albeit still slowly and fraught with wariness. The trees and bushes were in early bloom. It was beautiful, but we both sneezed, and our eyes ached. The one day I felt the need for extra fitness at the Claremont, I left Bob's cell phone with him and carried mine, so I could check in when I wanted. It did not stop the fear that an ambulance would be out front when I returned. I didn't know what to do about my anxiety. I didn't know how much to tell Bob. Each day, his anxiety seemed to decrease while mine raged on. Should I see a professional? Try anti-depressants? Talk to Marilyn? I auditioned each option in my mind until I found a reason to reject it, and then I'd start over.

When Bob had been well, he had been responsible for his own lunches. Now I made them. We grocery shopped together, but I was the one who kept an extra-cautious eye on what went in the cart. We had our first lunch out, splitting a chicken club sandwich, with an extra salad, and went to Berkeley Espresso, a café which I preferred to the French, because it was quieter and more spacious. I read and Bob wrote.

When he had finished, he asked about my writing. I had been working on Mold Central, a fictionalized memoir about the Home-into-Hell construction project we were in the throes of. It had begun when a plumber, called in to repair a burst water heater, had discovered fungus on our cellar walls. The water-damage restoration team staged a Haz-Mat suited, sci-fi-like invasion to seal the damaged area of our house tight before treating it with toxic chemicals to destroy the creatures the dampness had birthed, then had reported extensive dry rot lay beneath them. The repair work that had unleashed had visited delays upon us like still-continuing Biblical plagues. My tone, which mixed black humor with outrage, had helped me oversee this massive intrusion. But since Bob's heart attack, the emotional freedom to think hostile thoughts and fantasize revenge upon our contractor, felt dangerous. I'd long been vulnerable to thinking fate would punish me for anger, like I'd been genetically endowed with a permeable barrier that allowed thoughts to trigger retaliatory actions.

I told Bob I was having trouble resuming and that I was hungry for publication, especially at The Sun, a journal biased toward positive human experiences to difficult situations. It used to publish my pieces but had turned down my last four offerings.

"What have you learned from the events you're describing?" Bob said.

"One catastrophe flows from another?"

"Fair enough," Bob said. "'...but not for The Sun.'" Which directly quoted my last rejection from it.

He was right. There was probably a way to fit their taste by changing my tone, but in my current mood, even writing a hopeful sentence in my journal seemed beyond me.

Our first appointment with Dr. Fleur was February 14. Her group's office was on the fourth floor of a medical building, kitty-corner to Alta Bates. The suite's door listed eight names. She was the sole woman.

Adele and I already liked her. Her spirit and command in the ER had eased the uneasable. My primary treater, Harold Zipp, a perpetually smiling, nearly glowing, unreconstructed '60s guy, who at various times had counseled chanting, sweat lodges, and striving to become multiply orgasmic. Recently he had put me on a regimen of nutrients and supplements, including "taurine," "megapan" and "selenium," and had me regularly send a lock of hair to a Canadian laboratory for analysis. It concluded I was low in zinc, calcium and magnesium, and high in aluminum and cadium. (When I'd mentioned that Wikipedia said nothing more reassuring about what he was prescribing than "Of no proven medical benefit," Harry had replied "You want studies? I'll give you studies.") When Dr. Fleur heard what I was taking, she'd said, "If you want me to be your doctor, you have to stop them all." I had always been a patient who did as instructed, and since Harry had failed to guarantee me invincibility, I had shifted allegiance.

While I'd been in the hospital, Dr. Fleur had prescribed a half-dozen medications. They lowered cholesterol and blood pressure. They thinned blood and blocked betas. They encouraged me to pee, which, by reducing my water retention and, hence, my weight, made it easier for my heart to move me around. One pill staved off the indigestion the other pills might cause, and one the constipation.

The angina poster on the wall of the examining room commanded my attention. The illustrations of diseased arteries, congestive heart failure, even the healthy heart models, seemed like ghoulish fare on Valentine's Day.

I find doctors' appointments difficult in the best of times. From the minute they are scheduled, I lose my grip on life. In medical offices my blood pressure is off the charts. I feel even more anxious afterwards, if there are test results to wait for. I once confided in a doctor that I would rather be dead than there. "You shouldn't have to feel like that," he said. This concern did not match the ogre in my head. After that our appointments went better.

But Dr. Fleur was lovely, friendly and optimistic, and the room became less threatening.

One mystery that remained to be solved was what had gone wrong with me.

Heart disease is common enough. It kills more Americans than guns or cancer or motor vehicles. It kills a million of us each year. It kills more of us than anything. It kills when plaque build-up on interior arterial walls, or plaque ruptures, or a clot cuts off the flow of blood to the heart, starving it of oxygen, so tissue dies. Heart attacks killed Mama Cass and Elvis. F. Scott Fitzgerald and William Faulkner. Eldridge Cleaver and Lyndon Johnson. Lucky Luciano and Adlai Stevenson. But I had seemingly been free of risk factors. "If I can't find the reason," Dr. Fleur said, "my colleagues and I will have to change everything we've been doing."

She hoped Berkeley HeartLab would have the answer. It was one of the few labs in the country whose blood sample analyses go beyond merely reporting the levels of HDL (high density lipoprotein, or "Good" cholesterol) and LDL (low density lipoprotein, or "Bad" cholesterol). Such analyses often fail to identify those with coronary artery disease. But HeartLab's test costs $250, which most insurance plans will not cover, so most doctors do not order such analyses for their patients. These doctors then lack the findings which might alert them to conditions which could be treated before they progress to the point – like heart attacks – where even more expensive procedures are required.

I could afford $250. And when Dr. Fleur had the results, she could devise a treatment plan for me. First, though, my partially blocked artery had to be stented. "It will be simple," Dr. Fleur said. "They won't be operating under emergency conditions this time. And they have a road map to follow. It should take an hour."

I had already heard so many success stories about stents I believed they should test for them at seniors' athletic competitions, like steroids. My favorite was the ninety-two-year-old partner of a friend of Marilyn's who'd taken the friend to lunch the afternoon his went in. ("I'll beat that," I'd said to Adele. "I'll work out.") But I had also read a booklet from Alta Bates about post-operative care. "What about 'Walk five-to-ten minutes'?" I said. "'Lift no more than ten pounds'? Aren't I a heart attack *victim*? From now on, isn't that me?"

"They are not talking about you," Dr. Fleur said. "You are not massively obese. You do not smoke. You are basically a healthy man. In six months, you'll feel better than you did before. You probably did not realize how your restricted blood flow was affecting you. And you should believe everything I tell you, because I passed my boards two days ago."

Until the stenting occurred and my blood results were received, I could walk – but not uphill. I could use the treadmill – but no faster than I walked outside. I could ride a stationary bike – without resistance. Double espressos – even the occasional burrito – were fine. Dr. Fleur offered to place me on disability, but I preferred working, so we compromised on a few hours a day and, to avoid stress, no trials for sixty days. I received a card for my wallet in case my stent set off metal detectors.

"What about sex?" I said.

"Men," she said, turning to Adele.

Masturbation was fine.

"You were this close," Dr. Fleur had said at one point, pinching her thumb and index finger together until there was barely space between. The phrase "widow-maker" had entered the conversation.

21

III. NORMAL

The reassuring nature of Berkeley HeartLab's name was somewhat compromised by its being situated in an industrial park in Alameda. It was grander than the Lab Corp or Quest branches to which Adele and I were accustomed, but there was nothing on the premises that made us feel we were in the future. Neither the architecture or furniture were out of *Blade Runner*. The staff drew my blood with the usual sting and left the usual abused vein to remind me I had been there.

On our way to HeartLab, I felt we had come through a storm, a tornado out-of-season. Bob was not yet supposed to drive, so I was at the wheel. I was fine on city streets, but freeways made me shaky, and you had to enter Alameda through a tunnel, traffic rushing in the opposite direction, which felt an equivalent. Bob put a hand on my knee and said, "You're doing fine," but I wasn't. My heart was racing, and I felt faint. I remembered the time I'd been unable to change lanes on a freeway and had come to a stop and sat there in a full panic, with trucks barreling by on both sides, expecting to die.

I calmed down when we emerged, but I'd strained muscles in my neck and ground my teeth in an attempt to keep from exploding. We got lost when we turned right instead of left and had to double back, but made it to the appointment on time.

For the trip home, Bob insisted on driving to and through the tunnel. I didn't argue. Just before we reached the entrance, we were surprised by a hail barrage that melted as it hit the car. But out the other end, a rainbow lay ahead. I was into reading omens, and this one seemed to recapitulate the past month. In spite of the panic in the tunnel – and our life – we were recovering.

Alta Bates had notified Dr. Zipp of my admission, and he wanted to see me. His office was on an avenue of restaurants and gift shops, running east to west, from the flat lands by the bay to the hills, on the Berkeley-Albany border. He was friendly, concerned, and, aside from noting Dr. Fleur's "rigid" thinking, showed no signs of bruised feelings when he learned I'd jettisoned his supplements. He recommended that I continue Vitamin D and folic acid. (Dr. Fleur approved the former, with the endorsement, "I guess it can't do any harm" – and nixed the latter.)

The most surprising thing Dr. Zipp said was to finger work stress as a perpetrator of my undoing. I had prided myself on the healthy way I practiced law. I handled fewer cases and worked fewer hours than any work comp specialist I knew. I sought resolutions through smiles, not shouts, and compromise, not conflict. I might not make the money or attain the prominence of others, but, I felt, I went about things more wisely. I knew younger practitioners who'd had heart attacks, and I'd taken my avoiding them as confirmation my approach had inoculated me. Now I had to reconsider that wisdom.

In truth, I'd known my psyche was a problem. When some lawyers lost a case, it was the fault of an idiot judge or asshole client or sleazy defense attorney. With me, it was mine. I worried and re-worried each decision made, each step taken. Once Harry had spoken, I knew each lingering second-guess had cemented another blocking particle into my vessels.

I wondered what else I had mis-evaluated, beside my law practice. I recalled how I had begun catching an extra breath when I made my turn for the next lap in the pool. I recalled how the hills I'd walked once a week with my friend Robert, a glass artist, had seemed to grow more difficult to climb. I had explained it internally as age or deconditioning. Now I accused myself of having blindly walked – and swum – into this predicament.

"Breath the air," he said as I left. "Smell the flowers. Fondle Adele – and yourself."

Adele drove me to the office each morning and picked me up before noon. After lunch, we either went to the Claremont – where I avoided the pool – or for a walk, followed by a sit at the French, a short double espresso for me, a decaf, non-fat cap for her. Late afternoon and evenings, we'd watch a TV movie, tennis, of which Adele was a rabid fan, the Warriors, who were more my speed, or an episode from a cable series we followed.

The walks – on or off the treadmill – lengthened from ten- to twenty-five to thirty-five minutes. I thought less about my twinges. I experienced longer periods of not feeling at risk. The shaved hair of my groin did not grow back completely, but the swath of black-and-blue around the incision cleared.

I felt, I wrote in my journal, "almost normal."

I still felt frightened but less depressed, because I was doing something important, taking care of Bob.

I enjoyed our continued talks about writing. They gave me confidence in my ability to think through problems, other than how to make food interesting without salt. I re-wrote the first ten pages of Mold Central and wondered if they were good enough to send out.

I stopped worrying so much about his using the bathroom at night. Although I still awakened, I watched from the bed, occasionally falling back asleep before he returned. But sometimes I lay awake, disturbed by acid reflux or worried about incipient nosebleeds which stress drew from me. To pass the time, I'd mentally list what we'd need for our hospital overnight. The last time, stranded with nothing, I'd found a Tums in my jacket lining and rationed it.

We were both antsy, waiting for the stenting. Bob's feeling good was wonderful but made it harder to believe in its necessity. We wished for a he-didn't-have-to-do-it stage, not a trying-to-get-to-the-other-side-of-it stage.

Alta Bates had only one cath lab, so Dr. Fleur had sent Bob to Summit Hospital, on Oakland's Pill Hill, which had five. We spent the morning before there for pre-op testing, learned where to park and where to go when we entered. We ate lunch out, took a walk, and went to the French. After dinner, Bob packed his computer bag with books and writing. I filled my back pack with medicines, flashlight, toothbrush, a book, and a change of underpants, socks, slippers, and a sweatshirt for each of us. We each took an Ambien to help us sleep.

IV. ENTER THE PLUMBER

The stenting was scheduled for March 2, the day before Adele's birthday, which seemed to unnecessarily test the cosmos's ration of dark humor.

We parked on the garage's top floor, which was the same level as the reception area, the operating theaters, and the waiting room. After registering, I was assigned one of a dozen beds, separated into curtained off cubicles, on the perimeter of the pre-op/post-op room. From its center, nurses monitored each patient as if we were TV shows with competing plots to follow. I undressed and put on hospital clothes. Adele waited with me while I was worked up. A middle-aged Asian man was wheeled off on a gurney toward his episode's conclusion. To our right, the victim of palpitations while under evaluation for spinal surgery awaited results of that plot point's twist.

Dr. Tao, the "plumber" of Dr. Fleur's group, would operate. When he introduced himself, he told us that he might not be able to remove the blockage as planned and, if he couldn't, a more complicated approach might take two hours – and might require my receiving more than one stent. The problem was that my "lesion" encompassed both branches of the fork of a Y. (This was the first time we had heard that term. We much preferred "blockage.") "But," he said, "it's not twenty years ago and the Wild West, when they didn't know what they were doing. Now these things are routine, which is good." He paused before adding, "You don't want to be the exciting case."

Bob was taken off at 10 a.m., as planned, and I obediently went to the waiting room. His clothes remained in his cubicle and would accompany him to his room on the ward after he was returned there from surgery. Someone would get me when he was in post-op.

I had permission to call my sister Sylvia in Newton, a Boston suburb, and Marilyn, at any time, on their cell phones. Their availability felt good, but I planned to wait on my own and call when it was over. It was different this time. Bob was not in the middle of a heart attack. As Dr. Fleur had said, they knew where to go and what to do.

When I rolled into the operating room, a female singer whose pleasant voice I did not recognize, was coming through a loud speaker. "Who's that?" I said.

"Adele," the attendant said.

I found that comforting.

I was conscious throughout. (I had received a mild sedation but refused offers for more.) From the conversations between Dr. Tao, the nurse, Carol, and the technician, Patti, who were both beside the operating table, and Jules, who manned the fluoroscope from an elevated compartment to my left, it seemed a picture-transmitting probe had been inserted into my groin and conducted upward toward my blockages. It revealed, the Op Report later informed me, that my LCA had a "complex lesion… involving 3 major OM vessels as well as the AV groove circ forming a quadruple bifurcation lesion."

Dr. Tao tried to clear the blockages with balloons alone. That didn't work. He had to use stents. The first stent seemed to go in easily. But the second… There was an "inability to deliver" it. There was "significant resistance." Attempt after attempt proved "unsuccessful."

By turning my head, I could see the clock on the wall. I felt no pain or discomfort, except in my low back from having to continually lie supine, arms pressed against my sides. After two hours, Dr. Tao asked how I was doing.

"Fine," I said. "How're things going?"

"Fine," he said.

"Can someone tell my wife?" It might not be the Wild West to the professionals, but, for us amateurs, it was easier to believe in cures from newt eyes and bat wings than cameras traveling from groins to hearts, relaying pictures. I was trying not to worry and did not want Adele to. Worry would not change anything.

Not much later, Carol said, "She's fine."

I tried reading the first hour but ended up pacing after forty-five minutes. I didn't want to stray far, but after an hour and a half, I realized they had moved on to the longer solution. I felt a rush of fear.

I continued to walk. When it passed the two-hour mark, I did some stretches and tried to calm myself. A nurse arrived ten minutes later. "They'll be just a little longer," she said. I was shaking as she talked. She asked if I'd be more comfortable waiting in the recovery room. She brought me a cup of herbal tea. I was very grateful. She called the operating room, so they could tell Bob I was okay and waiting for him.

At hour three, Dr. Tao asked again how I was doing, and I again asked him how things were.

Before that, though, Dr. Tao and Jules had discussed approaching the "Y" through an entirely different blood vessel, and I had lain there attempting to impose the meditation mantra "Follow your breath... Follow your breath..."

It led to thoughts of when Adele and I met. The improbability of our connection had always seemed to me to border on the miraculous, and it seemed a good time to remind myself that miracles happened. It had been in a creative writing class at Brandeis University, my junior year, her senior. We dated the last weeks of that spring, the first months of the fall. Then she had dumped me and moved to San Francisco. We had been an unlikely couple. She was of the green book bag/black turtleneck set; and I was, if not a jock, a jock symp. She had been courted by the lead in *Sergeant Musgrave's Dance*, the heir to a cosmetics fortune, and the fellow who had led the picketers to the Watertown arsenal. I could barely talk to a girl unless alcohol had turned me charming. The first time I was primed to ask her to a party, she arrived for class in a Persian lamb jacket, looking like she was about to step out with Porfirio Rubirosa. That set me back several weeks. When I did finally ask her out, to hear Pete Seeger, she called me two hours before his show and said, "You won't believe me, but I am psychologically incapable of going on a date. For months, I wouldn't make one. Now I make – but break them."

There are moments in movies when someone points a gun at someone. The person at whom the gun is pointed has an instant within which to make a decision and act. If his decision is correct, he is the hero. If is decision is mistaken... "Let's not call it a date," I said. "I'll come by around 7:00. Then we'll walk down to the gym."

How did I ever think of that?

When we'd broken up, my heart had shattered. I had never met anyone like Adele. She knew about LSD; she played first singles on the tennis team; a photographer had asked her to pose, allegedly for *Playboy* (until he discovered she was sixteen); her Psychoanalysis and Literature paper on *The Stranger* had received A+. My first year at Penn Law School, I received a letter from Berkeley proposing we marry and join the Peace Corps. I played it cool, waited a week to reply, and did not hear from her again.

During the three years the country rocked to "Turn on; tune it; drop out," "Burn, baby, burn," "Hell, no, we won't go," I thought about Adele. Still needing a draft deferment after graduating, I joined VISTA, which sent me to Chicago's South Side to lawyer for street gangs. After six weeks, I jumped in a car with two pals to check out the Bay Area, post Summer of Love. And when I found Adele, she took me on a picnic on Mt. Tamalpais, with cheese, wine, sourdough bread – and pot. We stayed in touch through Martin Luther King's murder and Robert Kennedy's and the Chicago police beating demonstrators into the mud of Lincoln Park during the Democratic Convention. When my tour ended, I came back.

By the time the second stent was in place, Dr. Tao had ordered his next scheduled patient returned to his cubicle. I needed a third.

The pressure the two new stents had added on the artery had combined with that from the two already in place to make positioning a fifth even more difficult. Dr. Tao and Jules debated different sizes for this or that. They debated matters that escaped me. At times my gurney shook like the doctor was trying to hammer the stent into position, one-quarter millimeter by one-quarter millimeter. Part of me thought, Stay calm. They will get this. But a corner prepared for, "We're sorry. We did all we could."

After four hours, a perspiring Dr. Tao exclaimed, "An excellent result!" He winked. "You were the exciting case after all." He rushed off to tell Adele.

Patti and Carol were excited too. First, they showed me a stent. (It was humbling to see I was running only because of several what-appeared-to-be ballpoint pen springs.) Then they insisted Jules put pictures on the screen so I could view my artery "Before" and "After." I had no idea what I was looking at. But I knew I was going home the next morning with a new phase of life with which to engage.

The whole damned thing was amazing.

After calling to say they were finished and he was washing up, Dr. Tao arrived to draw me a pen-and-ink picture of what they'd accomplished. It looked like a seventy-five-car pile-up had turned into a smooth-running freeway.

"With all the plaque and calcification, you'd have thought a bomb had gone off in there," he said.

I gave him a big hug and thanked him.

I had a smile on my face when Bob arrived in post-op – and he had one for me. After his vitals had stabilized, they wheeled him into an elevator, upstairs to the heart ward. We were in a four-patient room, across from the nurses. I began lobbying for a private, so I could spend the night.

We called friends. Bob read the newspaper and watched TV, waiting for his "Don't-move-your-leg-for-six-hours" to pass. He ate his first meal; then they transferred us to a private room. It took a few hours to find me a cot, and, again, it was a horror. Broken springs jutted through a thin mattress.

I wondered if this was a device designed by hospital administrative directors to drive meddlesome family members home. I added several blanket layers beneath me, but I still felt like I was sleeping on antlers.

The morning brought new worries. Bob's blood pressure was so low they thought he might need transfusions. But after breakfast and two walks around the floor, it rose sufficiently for us to go home. Though Bob had to be transported from the room in a wheelchair, the attendant let him walk down a few steps to our car in the lot.

By the time we got home, Bob had a fever and chills. I called the hospital and was told the fever should subside by morning, but if it spiked, I should bring him back. We had a light supper, some relaxed moments, and slept.

V. WHAT AM I DOING HERE?

Berkeley HeartLab answered Dr. Fleur's question.

Heart disease is not simply a matter of HDLs, LDLs, and triglycerides, she explained at our next visit. Cholesterol breaks down into a dozen components; and even if your gross numbers are fine, interaction between a sub-component and your genes, or clotting mechanism, or inflammatory process may be pernicious. One of my components had been surreptitiously transforming what registered as "Good" into "Bad." What was supposed to be too "big" to do me damage was, in actuality, "small," and my arteries had clogged.

A gene had done me in.

"A simple fix," Dr. Fleur said.

She directed me to a twelve-week, thirty-six-session cardiac-rehabilitation program. She added Niaspan to my medications. That made a dozen: Lipitor, Plavix, Toprol, Tramadol, Metoprolol, Aldactone, Ativan, Lexapro, Prasugrel, Digoxin, Ramipril, and it.

Isn't Niaspan in Rice Krispies, I thought. Could I change breakfast instead?

"It may itch," she said. "So take it before you go to sleep."

Cardio-rehab was in a one-story, cinderblock building, within sight of Alta Bates, across from a Whole Foods. Before I could begin, I had to meet with a nurse for orientation.

"What are your goals?" she asked.

"Spiritual transformation," I said.

She looked at me.

"I thought the idea was not to have goals," I said.

"We'll say 'Fulfilling the exercise standards.'"

Now I had to wait for a slot to open.

While I waited, I worried. I worried about angina and embolisms. I worried if my flimsy-seeming stents would fail and if having had one heart attack left me more vulnerable to a second.

My groin still ached. So did the left side of my chest. I needed Ambien to sleep. Going up or down our front steps left me dizzy. Adele would not let me take walks alone, or carry groceries, or drive the car.

I bristled at such "controls," but I did my part. Twenty years earlier, when I had been diagnosed with borderline high blood pressure, Dr. Zipp had recommended a course on "Mindfulness," as a way to reduce my feeling stressed. It had helped. My blood pressure had come down, and I had continued to meditate, twenty to thirty minutes a day. I was not a "good" meditator, a judgment whose existence alone probably proved the point, but I had kept on my desk a copy of *Zen Mind, Beginner's Mind* for reinforcement. I turned to it now.

"Nothingness" did not comfort me, but "Forgiveness" – especially of my self -- seemed worth striving for.

My first day of rehab, in the first conversation I overheard, a man was telling two others about landing with the Eighth Army, in Japan, two weeks after Hirohito had surrendered. All three had fifteen years on me, minimum. What am I doing here? I thought.

Most of those in my dozen-member class were male and white. I was older than a few but appeared better conditioned than almost everyone. Arrhythmia had brought some and M.I.s others; some were post-bypass or other major surgery.

Before each session, we attached six electrodes to our chest. To each electrode, we snapped on a wire, which connected to a battery-powered monitor nestled within a pouch slung over our necks. Then, rigged so the monitors would enable staff nurses to oversee our hearts' rhythms while we exercised, we waited on a slatted bench for our blood pressures to be taken. There was little chit-chat. People were nervous. People were private. Once a week, we were weighed.

Each class opened with ten minutes of instructor-led warm-up stretches and aerobic exercises. Then we rotated through ten-minute stints on each of three different machines. Some did a rowing or elliptical machine, but the treadmill, stationary and recumbent bikes were mine. Midway through, the staff checked our blood pressure again. "Work at a level that requires effort," they told us, "but don't become uncomfortable." "Exercise on three of your days off, but allow your body to recover on the fourth." Each class ended with ten minutes of cool-down stretches. Once a week was a half-hour class: diet; stress reduction; heart-disease-and-you.

I increased my pace and the levels of resistance of the machines. I exercised at the Claremont on my off days. I met each goal the staff set for me. When a nurse referred to the damage my heart had suffered as "minimal," my confidence increased. Friends exhibited less concern about me; no longer being a center of attention caused me no distress. Each person's "graduation" from cardio-rehab was announced and applauded. I looked forward to mine.

But some people disappeared, mid-program, without a word. And there was always someone to replace whoever left.

One day short of two months after my heart attack, while leaving my tenth rehab session, I felt pain in my chest. It was different than my prior pain – but not different enough. I got in my car but did not start it. I had set personal bests on all three machines that morning. I cursed myself for having over-done it and made apologies and promises to God.

I sat for some minutes. The pain remained the same. I called Adele and told her without explanation I might be late for lunch. I re-entered the building. My heartbeat was slow. My blood pressure — 97/50 — was low. (120:70 is normal.) I asked a nurse if I should try a nitro. She thought that a good idea.

I began to lose consciousness, I lay on the slatted bench. There was a burning sensation in my chest. I felt clammy to the touch. An EKG showed my heart was contracting improperly. Someone called 911. Somewhere in there I puked. The last thing I remember is a paramedic saying, "We're going to have to cut this shirt off you, sir."

VI. I DON'T KNOW

Until that Wednesday, I had never let Bob go to cardio-rehab without me. I would hang around while he was there, sometimes copying down recipes from the healthy-eating cookbooks that looked good and not too hard. Or I'd take a walk, or pick up groceries at Whole Foods, or go to the Claremont for a quick work-out and shower. Rehab wouldn't let me use its machines because if I fell, its insurance wouldn't cover me.

But I'd decided I'd been holding us both back out of an unreasonable fear that something untoward would happen if we were apart. I'd recognized how controlling and "controlled" I'd been, how the two went together and boxed out the fresh air of autonomy and choice. So I'd let him give our vintage Mustang an airing and go alone. I was nervous but tried to take advantage of the luxury of free time, slowly prepping our lunches and savoring the play at the Miami Masters tennis tournament. Bob had said he'd call me on my cell when he was ready to leave.

Re-taking previously occupied areas of autonomy interrupted by trauma has always been treacherous for me. I'd learned to crawl, walk, and run under the graphic verbalizations of the horrors they could result in from my mother, who'd been plagued most of her life by mental and physical ills and a myriad of fears. When I'd been a child, my baby carriage rides were often interrupted by her screams when she'd spotted a dog in the distance and roughly snatched me up to carry me into an apartment building until it had passed. When I was an adolescent, the dangers of boys who drove red sports cars had become paramount.

In my marriage, without her daily reminders of disaster, I'd developed from feeling vulnerable every moment to sometimes thinking of Bob and I as invulnerable. The heart attack had knocked that askew, and a dark cloud had formed around me. I was fearful of the need to do the things Bob used to do. But I would do whatever was necessary to take care of both of us. If he died, I'd find a way to follow him. It seemed strange it was he who had become vulnerable and not I.

While I'd awaited Bob's call, I'd kept watch of the time and kept busy, only occasionally experiencing an eruption of anxiety. But when his call didn't come when expected, I felt a jolt of fear.

Maybe he forgot, I thought. Maybe he had a car accident. Maybe he had been done in by the no-cooking-for-me burrito I had let him pick up for dinner the night before. I checked my cell in case I'd missed a message. About ten minutes into my worries, it rang. Bob didn't sound bubbly like he usually did after a session.

I was too frightened to ask if something was wrong. Instead I said, "Do you want chicken or tuna on your salad?" When he said to hold off on lunch until he got home, I became annoyed. As soon as we hung up, I wanted to call back and start over.

The anxiety had made me sweat and smell, so I showered.

As I was drying off, the phone rang. A nurse from cardio-rehab was half-way through leaving a message, when I grabbed the phone and made her start over. Bob had collapsed from a heart attack, and an ambulance had arrived. He was conscious, but they were leaving for the ER at Summit momentarily.

I asked if I could speak to Bob. She said, "No. The medics are working on him. You can meet him at the ER."

I threw on clothes, grabbed my backpack, and drove to Summit. I was terrified. I felt an unspoken rage that my pleasures of the morning had led to this disaster. If I'd gone with Bob, at least we would be together. Any progress made with my baby steps toward autonomy had been gutted.

I went the same route the ambulance would have, but I couldn't catch up.

I pulled into the ER parking lot and ran inside. I was escorted to where Bob was being readied for surgery. It was nothing like the first attack. He was an ashen, thousand-year-old man.

We held hands as long as we could. "I'll be waiting when you wake up," I said. "You'll be fine."

"I don't know," he said.

They were the saddest, most forlorn words I'd ever heard. I felt cold through and through.

"I love you so much," I said.

He said the same.

They rushed him to surgery.

I followed the gurney. When told where I had to wait, followed some more – but further behind. I turned a corner in time to see the operating theater they entered.

I sat nearby on the floor. I paced the hall. More doctors arrived. Then an alarm sounded. "ALL AVAILABLE DOCTORS TO SURGERY ONE," screamed the loud speakers. "CODE BLUE."

I thought Bob was dying.

I prayed.

In my head, I screamed "Noooooooo!"

A cart of resuscitation equipment arrived. Three more doctors entered. I perched at the edge of the worst feelings I had ever had, my heart drumming, bells in my ears, trying to catch my breath and keep my breakfast down. I imagined dying myself, before even hearing if Bob had survived. I remained seated so I'd have less distance to fall.

When the cart came out and I was told Bob was alive, I said, "Thank you."

A while later, a woman in a pleated skirt and floral blouse came out of a nearby office to ask what I was doing there. When I told her, she gently invited me in and offered me a seat. She brought me a bottled water and a cup. She called for an update and told me the doctors were doing all they could and knew where I was. I thanked her for her kindness.

She suggested I call someone to be with me. I explained that I felt the best chance of me and Bob surviving was for me to keep the vigil by myself. I felt in a sacred place within myself, able to keep away from vanishing over the precipice of fear and hold onto the hope, the possibility, that when I did call my family and friends, I would be able to say we had come through, not unscathed, but alive.

I'd been there an hour when a doctor I'd never seen before – tall, pale, sixty-ish, in surgical whites – came to speak with me. He told me that the heart attack had been "massive" and that Bob's life remained in danger. They were continuing to work on him, but he couldn't promise Bob would survive.

I wondered why he'd bothered, if that was all he had to say. I closed my eyes and tried to recover.

Of all my waits at hospitals, this was the worst. Bob's last "I don't know" echoed.

The next two doctors to visit, an hour apart, looked like the first, except one had a mustache and one wore glasses. Neither offered anything hopeful. The woman in the office, Anne, again encouraged me to call someone. I thought about it. I could hear each person's voice, their concern, their offers to help. I wasn't ready for any of that. I wanted Bob.

I paced the halls. I had a cup of chamomile tea. Anne offered me a banana and I took a few bites. Bob had not coded again, and I took that as a good sign. When Anne left for business in another part of the hospital, we hugged.

Late afternoon, a doctor, who'd aged years since I'd seen him earlier, a haggard composite of all the doctors, said they were done. Bob was alive -- and now had seven stents. It would be touch-and-go for the next twenty-four to forty-eight hours. He would be in a drug-induced coma, in the third-floor ICU, on life-support. It would take an hour to get him settled. Then I could see him.

It wasn't great news, but it was infinitely better than the worst news. I called my brother Gordie, in Amherst, and sister. I called Marilyn, who said she and Griff, her husband, would come, and I could sleep at their house if I wanted. When I said I was definitely sleeping at the hospital, she said they'd come anyway, and I could decide after I'd seen Bob. It felt good to have a few people who cared about us knowing where we were. I moved the Honda from the ER parking lot into the hospital's.

According to the medical records, this is what had happened.

I had arrived in the Cath Lab "in cardiogenic shock." My blood pressure was 60/40, which meant my heart was not pumping blood with sufficient force to my organs. I was in danger of kidney failure, a stroke, death. An angiogram showed my LAD had re-clotted. My LCA was blocked as well. Dr. Tao was again in charge of fixing me.

He began with the LCA. The first wire he tried could not penetrate the occlusion. Neither could a larger one. The third did – but could not remove the clot. Then he tried a balloon, which couldn't get through – and caused a "loss of wire position."

Dr. Tao turned to the LAD. On his second attempt, he cleared some of the clotted material, but another angiogram revealed that one of my prior stents, further in, was now ninety percent closed. Since he had some flow going though, he returned to the LCA. He was able to get a wire in, and a balloon established a partial flow there.

But the LAD had re-occluded. After two attempts, a catheter got it flowing too. At this point, Dr. Tao asked a surgeon about performing a bypass, but the surgeon believed me "too sick" to withstand one. Dr. Tao went back to my LAD. He positioned a new stent, so that it partially overlapped my old one. He "hit" this with a balloon stent and "deployed" another across the ninety percent blockage. A final angiogram showed "a reasonable flow down the LAD." Now he re-engaged with the LCA. A wire got a flow going; a stent established this flow as "normal."

Meanwhile, a balloon pump, inserted into my aorta by way of another catheter, had raised my blood pressure slightly. Drip infusions of two medications failed to raise it more, but it was good enough to wheel me out of there. I still needed work on other blockages, but that was enough for now.

It had taken four hours. "Excellent angiographic results," was Dr. Tao's conclusion.

The ICU had a locked door. My call on the phone beside it rang several times before a woman answered. I said that my husband had recently arrived from surgery. She said someone would get me within the hour.

The waiting room was directly across from the ICU. It held couches and chairs and coffee tables. Families sat hunched together, talking. People slept sitting up or sprawled on a couch. A TV hung from a corner wall, beside a clock. At the far end of the room, one family had grouped couches and chairs together to form a private place. Backpacks, blankets and coolers secured their space until their owners returned.

I sat facing the door with the phone. The entire area was glassed in, and people and gurney traffic passed by. Bob would have journeyed from the operating theater past where I sat. The thought made me feel at home. Doctors in surgical scrubs arrived and talked with individuals and families. Some looked relieved and some not.

The hour passed. I called into the ICU again. This time, they buzzed me through. I signed in at the nurse's station, gave my contact information, and someone took me to the cubicle where Bob lay. Tubes coming out of his mouth and neck and chest connected him to life support machines and monitors. Restraints kept his arms from tearing out any of the lines. I was allowed to sit beside his bed. I put my hand on his. From time to time, I stood and stretched and went to the bathroom. Nurses came in and out. I felt better, but still petrified.

I'd called cardio-rehab after the operation to bring them up to date. They had placed a note on the Mustang, asking it not be towed. When Marilyn and Griff arrived, I gave them the keys, so one of them could drive it to their house. I resisted their offer to stay with them, even when they promised to drive me back to the hospital at the crack of dawn or if called in the middle of the night.

I wanted to stay as close to Bob as possible. I didn't think I could survive if I didn't.

After his night nurse said she would get me if Bob woke and that, if I woke first, I could visit him, I agreed to sleep in the waiting room. I pushed two chairs together at a distance from the people who had filled the saved space I'd noticed earlier. In the group's center was a beautiful young Indian woman in skinny-legged designer jeans and colorful embroidered blouse. Clustered around her were several friends and her father, who had brought them pizza and beverages, sandwiches, cupcakes, and chips. I took comfort from their laughter and talk and fell asleep, my head on a pillow the nurse had given me, a blanket over my clothes and jacket. I visited Bob three times during the night. It had been a good choice to stay.

In the morning, I cleaned up and chatted with the young woman. She had been sleeping there for a week and sitting with her mother every day, praying for her to come out of a coma. She spoke with religious fervor about the power of positive thinking and enlisted me to add her Mom to my prayers. In return she would pray for Bob. She invited me to join her group. I thanked her and felt I'd made a friend.

But arrangements to move her mother to a long term facility came through that afternoon. My friend and I hugged good-bye. She showed me how to claim my space by attaching a note to the blanket and pillow. I appropriated her couch, which had a good view of the corridor and was at the greatest distance from the TV, where most people tended to congregate. That night, a noisy bunch kept it on, while a parade of steadily arriving relatives and friends, all seemingly hearing challenged, heard the same long, sad story told loudly, over and over.

At midnight, I asked if the TV could be turned off and their voices lowered. A large man with a big belly and tiny mustache yelled that this room was for relatives of people in ICU. I said that was true, and that I was one too, and that I needed sleep. They turned the set off but not their voices down. I plugged my ears with cotton balls and slept on and off for a few hours.

That morning, watching a nurse give Bob a sponge bath, I was shocked by the changes in his body. His abdomen was rounded like a drum. His normally long, slender, well-muscled legs looked like balloons. His thin, angular face had filled out, so he looked decades younger. They were about to saw off his wedding ring, when Alison, his day nurse, said she could remove it. She layered on Vaseline until it slipped free. I washed it and strung it from a string of diamond slivers which has hung around my neck since I inherited it from my mother thirty years before. Alison assured me I was seeing 35 pounds of water retained from the fluids pumped into Bob to keep him alive during the surgery, and that in a few days he'd have his physique back.

Alison was a peach, efficient, smart and kind, with red hair and an athlete's lithe body.

"Bob is really going to like you," I said.

"He won't remember me," she said. "His memory of nurses will come and go, long after you are out of Intensive Care."

"Then I'll tell him about you when he can remember."

That afternoon Bob slightly tugged as I held his hand. It felt so good. He was making steps out of the coma. Sadly, he also moaned in distress.

Later, Margery, a heavy-set, forty-five-year-old from Social Services, stopped by. She'd be arranging a rehab facility for Bob after he left the hospital. It was difficult, she said, to get into one, and she wanted to begin working on it.

Instead of feeling reassured by her diligence, I was enraged. The doctor had not yet taken Bob off the critical list. He was still in Intensive Care. How could Margery dare to presume what Bob would need by the time he would leave the hospital? She then asked me a dozen worrisome questions about our house's stairs, railings, the distance from our bed to the bathroom, and the bathroom's safety features. I told her I'd have a handyman make safer what we could.

"You do what you believe necessary," I said, " but, when the time comes, we are going home.

After Marjorie left, there was an equally disturbing visit from a clergyman who "happened to be in the neighborhood."

That night, I reluctantly agreed to sleep at home. A night nurse had said that since Bob had passed the most critical period, it was time for me to take care of myself, so I'd be ready when he became more active. That made sense. I needed a shower, a better sleep, a change of clothes, my own vitamins and pills for the days ahead. I needed to go through the mail and pick up bills and the checkbook. I wasn't sure I should be driving in my current state; but finding the waiting room full, with a strong smell of sweat, anxiety, and unhappiness in the air, and rejecting bunking in the Honda, I set out on the journey.

Telegraph Avenue's traffic was light. I tried the classical music station, but the violins made me cry. I passed corner markets, open for the cigarette and alcohol trade, three funeral homes, and a crematorium. When I reached a stretch *of trendy restaurants, it felt like an oasis. People out for fun on a weekday night made it seem I had traveled a great distance.*

I relaxed my arms, which had clutched the wheel since I'd left the parking lot, and felt for my cell phone. I'd had a panicky thought that it was not on and that the hospital had tried to reach me. Imagining being out of touch, for even a few moments, had sent a chill up my spine. All the moments I'd felt relatively safe, the reassuring image of Bob asleep and watched over in my head, erupted into a series of imaginary crises. But the phone was on; there had been no calls.

As I braked for a red light, I tried to relax again. My foot slipped off the brake, tapped the accelerator, and the Honda slammed into the rear of a BMW convertible.

I got out, with registration and license in hand. I hoped the other driver wasn't hurt and that the damage wouldn't necessitate waiting for the police to write a report. She was in her late twenties, dressed for a night out in four-inch heels and a short and sparkly skirt. "I'm sorry," I said. "Are you okay?"

"I think so," she said, "but you look badly shaken."

I explained where I'd been for two days.

The BMW's dent wasn't bad. She opened and closed its trunk. "Let's forget it. I have a party to get to, and you need sleep."

I was shocked and grateful. She wished me and my husband good luck, and we hugged.

I imagined how much Bob would enjoy this story, when he was home and feeling better. I had my first smile in over forty-eight hours. I'd run into – literally – an angel.

As I drove home, I marveled at the mind's ability to open to the magical in ordinary encounters when the going is rough. When I'd been a child, my father's playfulness – tickling, licking, snuggling, – had over-stimulated my body and imagination. In response, I had become phobic, substituting other objects and activities for him, to keep myself from being overwhelmed. Dogs, which, though they sent my mother running, my father mimicked in his play, became a focus for my fears. I think now he was trying to initiate me into the world of excitement that was part of his nature, but then I mixed my parents' competing messages together. While he pinned me flat to the bed or floor, and my mother raged, "You'll drive her wild!", I became unable to tell the difference between fear and pleasure.

Then after my father had died, a puppy, which seemed to embody his sprightly gait, kept finding and following me, wagging its tail. The doggie's repeated appearances had helped me to face the loss of things I had loved about my father and to feel appreciated by him, as if he'd come to me in a form I could now manage and of which I no longer need be afraid.

And five years before that, after my mother had passed, I had been walking at Inspiration Point, atop a chain of hills that divides Berkeley from Contra Costa County, the late afternoon light reminding me of the celestial glow in Botticelli's faces, when I'd spotted an old friend, Dune Ellen, smoothing along the trail toward me, the first wisps of returning fog nipping at her heels. Opening both arms, she enfolded me into her velour jumpsuit, and something inside me switched on like a pilot light.

When I told her why I was walking, Dune's eyes scanned the sky, her orbs pale, flat, inside-out flying saucers. Since our falling out decades earlier – over Bob's scoffing at her husband Trey's reports of a medium's connecting them with the departed – they had made millions in the stock market, founded an institute for paranormal research on their Moraga ranch, and hosted conferences for spiritual leaders and titans of industry. I wondered what Dune saw.

"She's here," she said.

Just that – and I saw alphabet soup-size replicas of my mother. They pirouetted on the eucalyptus leaves; they floated in the air on motes of dust; they filled the too blue sky. Effortlessly, I moved from one image to another as one does on the way to sleep. The mother fragments formed a safety net. "Mother," I said, "I'm not angry anymore" and felt forgiveness in return.

Now I forgave myself for the anger I had felt when Bob called the morning of his heart attack, and eased the blame we impose on ourselves for the ills that strike those we love.

Inside the house, though, alone, it didn't feel so good. I turned up the heat and saw, in the refrigerator, Bob's partially prepared salad had frozen. I showered and climbed into bed, the cell phone on the pillow beside me. I hoped Bob was resting well. I prayed he would wake soon and find me by his bedside. I was, I sensed, becoming able to feel hopeful, to strengthen myself in order to help him to recover, and to adjust to the forthcoming changes in our life. I was collecting good talismans with which to meet the challenges of each day. I fell asleep on thoughts of kindnesses, big and small, from strangers, friends and family.

At 2:00 AM, a nurse called to ask permission to administer a transfusion to Bob. It was probably standard, but in the terror from having been suddenly awakened, I wanted the surgeon's reassurance before giving my okay. She said he was too busy to consult with me, so I called and woke Artie, an ER doctor in Napa, and friend of Bob's since college. He explained the procedure to me.

I told the hospital, "Yes." Artie had become another angel.

Sunday, Bob was awake on and off, but he had no short term memory. It was like the movie "Groundhog's Day," with me having many chances to catch him up on what had happened. He also conveyed how depressed he was.

While he napped, I went to the Claremont and found myself talking to Judy, a Reformed rabbi, who had just finished her aerobic workout. She suggested I have the doctor start Bob on anti-depressants and, if he balked, request a psych consult. Her husband, a psychiatrist, used them successfully with patients who'd had heart attacks, and she had seen the difference they made in people she counseled.

I took her advice back to Summit and Bob. He nodded his interest. Dr. Fleur was on vacation, and different doctors in her group had been attending Bob. An hour later, I had one on the phone, and he agreed to prescribe Prozac. (Upon her return, Dr. Fleur switched Bob to Lexapro. She liked, she later explained, to match anti-depressants to individuals. Prozac made people "anxious," which caused them to lose their appetites; so she prescribed it for her obese patients. But since Bob was thin, Lexapro seemed a better choice.) When Bob took his first dose, I didn't say it could take weeks to work, because sometimes just knowing help is on the way is enough.

Once his restraints were removed, Bob moaned and pointed to this throat. Alison repositioned his breathing tube, and the moaning stopped. But even after the tube was removed for good the following day, and Bob was breathing on his own, his coughing and gagging continued and became worse when he tried to swallow, even soft food or liquids. (We would learn that the insertion of the breathing tube during surgery had scratched one of his vocal chords. It had contracted, allowing foreign particles to enter his trachea. If he swallowed saliva – or a speck of dust – incorrectly, it unleashed a paroxysm of coughing.)

That night, I pulled two chairs together in the waiting room, fashioned a makeshift bed, and slept over.

In the morning, Bob was taken off the heart machine. He had lost all the water weight and then some. He was doing so well that his attending doctor wanted to schedule him for another Cath Lab session to ensure that his stents remained clear. Bob shook his head and tried to speak.

"I don't think he's ready for that," I said.

Bob took my hand and nodded.

"Sometime next week will be fine," the doctor said.

Before Alison left for the weekend, she introduced a way for Bob to communicate. First, she offered him a pen and paper, but he could not write. Then she handed him a pointer and a board with the letters of the alphabet affixed to it. He didn't make it through "Thank you"; but, over the next few days, his pointing became surer and faster. "Yes," "No," "Water," "OK," "I love you." A lot of "I love you"s. We enjoyed eye contact and holding hands. I could talk to him. But I feared his never being able to speak again.

I alternated nights at home and in the waiting room. I wept at each separation. Once I dreamt a surgeon said, "He didn't make it," and I died on the spot.

VII. FIVE YEARS AGO, YOU WOULD HAVE BEEN DEAD

The doctors had kept me from white-lighted tunnels at the ends of which deceased relatives wave "Welcome," but the first days I was conscious, coughing was only one of my problems. I had swallowed vomit at cardio-rehab, and contracted double pneumonia. I could barely eat or drink. I could not stand. I pissed into a tube and could not move my bowels. I couldn't concentrate enough to read or watch television. If I wrote in my journal, my handwriting went scribbly, minuscule, floated above and below the lines on the page. The tubes that connected me to the machines had locked me into lying on my back so long that a pulpy cyst, which had bulged benignly beside my spine for years, had become aggravated and burst, staining my gown with blood and puss and leaving me vulnerable to infection. The wound required cleaning and bandaging, twice daily, and was so sore I had to lie with an inflatable, plastic do-nut of a pillow encircling, but not touching, it. I was physically and emotionally drained. I dreamed I was surrounded by old friends who had become Russian agents and ran murderously amok.

I had done everything right; yet here I was again. I did not think I could go on, heart attacks crashing down upon me, unprovoked, any time, out of nowhere. Thinking how my acting upon this despair would affect Adele shamed me; but the idea crouched inside my head, wielding its potentially lethal pitchfork.

My tenth day in the ICU, they wheeled me back to the Cath Lab for a "look-see." Again, I have no memory of it, but this is what the Op Report says.

Dr. Tao used an IVUS, a miniature ultrasound probe, to tell him what was going on. He began with my LCA but ran into "some difficulty due to hanging on the stent struts." Two attempts to get by failed. His first attempt at a balloon angioplasty could not widen the passageway, but a second succeeded. Everything looked good, so he turned to my LAD. The IVUS showed an existing stent in "mild malposition" and "significant stenosis" elsewhere. A balloon corrected the stent's position and widened the flow. A new stent was implanted and dilated to address the narrowing.

The result was I "left the lab in stable position without chest pain" – and seven stents, which, I believe, tied the PAC-12 record.

I sat alone in the waiting room while Bob was in the Cath Lab. I paced, read, and received the good news from the doctor moments before Bob's gurney reappeared. He was awake; we kissed; and I followed him to Cardiac Intensive Care, our new residence, which was restricted to heart patients. The population was smaller than the ICU; but instead of each patient having a nurse, every two patients shared one. I went home each night, but we put in for a private room with a cot on the general cardiac ward, Bob's next step on the way home, so I could stay over.

The nurses were efficient but busier and less personal than those in ICU, changing each day and night, making it harder to establish relationships to get what you needed when you needed it. Once Alison popped in to see how Bob was doing. Later, when he was napping and she was at the front desk, I asked her about the damage to his heart. I quickly wished I hadn't. I buried the possible complications she foresaw and hoped for better luck.

Ann, whose office I'd shared while Bob had been in surgery, came by too. I barely knew her or she us, but feelings of connection and caring overwhelmed me. I told her I'd never forget her thoughtfulness. Bob, who, by now, had regained moments of consciousness, thanked her for taking care of me. When she left, I wanted to curl up in his arms, be held, and tell him everything that was bottled up inside me. We watched a few innings of an A's game, and when he fell asleep, I walked around the floor. The family room, at its far end, was equipped with computers, TV, tables, chairs, couches, and a mini-bar with free coffees, teas, fruit juices, apples, and bananas. I registered and received a name tag. There were two clean, spacious bathrooms. I used one, checked tennis scores on a computer, and wrote some e-mails. I knew I'd be back each day.

Friday afternoon, Bob and I awaited his transfer to the cardiac ward. We watched a pitchers' duel between the A's and Twins. The A's had led 1-0 since the first, but, in the eighth, Minnesota scored twice. Bob had just said, "Well, it's a long season," when they came to move us.

We had a private room on Sutter's southwest side. A cot was moved in for me. We were both much happier going to sleep and waking together. I'd leave for a portion of each day, pick up Bob's mail from his office and, the following day, deliver his responses to his secretary. I'd thought that the reason Bob's morning blood pressure registered low was that, by the time it was taken, he'd been up for hours with nothing to eat, so I'd keep yogurt and non-fat muffins on-hand for us. I had permission to use the staff's refrigerator and to raid the linen closet for extra blankets, towels and pillows as needed. The head nurse basically had said, "Treat this as your home while you are here."

The nurse-patient ratio was now one-to-four. All but one sourpuss were good, and a few were beyond excellent, adapting to our particular needs and involving me in Bob's care, so I'd be prepared for when we'd be home. Physical therapists were in short supply, but I kept lobbying for one; and, Sunday, shortly before noon, a sweet, young novice, named Bette, appeared. She used most of her time taking a medical history, which was already in Bob's chart. She didn't look strong enough to lift me, let alone him, but together we got Bob standing for a few wobbly steps in place.

She seemed in a hurry to leave once Bob's lunch arrived. I walked her out, asking about the schedule for the week. I breathed a sigh of relief when she said someone else would come the next day. Then she expressed concern about Bob's weakness and low blood pressure. She said she would recommend a rehab facility for when we left the hospital.

"He'll be much stronger in a week," I said, hoping I was right.

All I recall of that session is that, at Bette's direction, I changed my socks, lifted an arm overhead, walked ten steps in place.

"Excellent," she said.

How little I could do terrified me.

Monday, Heidi, tall, strong, with red hair and blue eyes, had Bob warm up in a seated position, by raising his legs and exercising his arms, before he walked in place. He proved so much steadier than the day before, she took him for a walk in the hall, while I rolled the oxygen stand and portable drips behind them. It was wonderful to see Bob upright, out in the world, albeit a hospital ward. When he was ready to turn back, she gave him tips on focusing and walking with a widened gait for better balance. He smiled at me and nodded at another patient making his way down the hall, alone, in the opposite direction.

In our room, Heidi said, "How did that feel?"

"I'm glad to be back in bed," Bob said. "But good."

"You can do that a couple more times today. A nurse should accompany you and Adele, but, in a day or two, you'll be free to walk together, whenever you wish."

She took his blood pressure. "Much better," she said.

One problem though was that the afternoon sun made our room unbearably hot. And jack-hammering from a construction project across from our window drove me crazy. I asked to transfer across the hall, and, two days later, we received the first room to free up. But soon after we moved in, our TV exploded, filling the room with acrid smoke, and we were evacuated.

Our third room was fine. I ditched my new cot's too-squeaky metal frame but kept the mattress and made my bed on the floor at the foot of Bob's.

Adele absorbed all the doctors said. She encouraged me with what should be encouraged and discouraged me from what should not be. If nurses did not respond to my buzz, she sought them. If they were late with pills, she pursued them. If their schedule did not match my needs, she hectored for alterations. She bussed away my trays as soon as I finished meals and made sure my water pitcher was full. She reminded the nurses when it was time to change the antibiotic feed and had them check drips that were not dripping.

Each night, she read to me from *Just Kids*, Patti Smith's memoir about her relationship with Robert Mapplethorpe. Though we knew his hideous end, their tenderness and commitment spoke to us. If the devil was in my head, Adele was the angel beside me.

One evening, a twenty-something nursing assistant remarked, "You must have been a fun couple when you were young."

"We were a fun couple when we were old," I said.

"We were a fun couple last Wednesday," Adele said.

I slept better. I read the sports section and watched the news. I sat up for an hour. I left a message on my office answering machine that my suitemate would be handling my cases. I knew I was done with the law. We had my IRA and Social Security. We owned our house and had no children and lived modestly.

I did not think about it beyond that.

Heidi gave Bob physical therapy every day. We walked further and more often. We exchanged smiles with other patients doing the same.

Bob had respiratory therapy every six hours. They'd check his oxygen levels, listen to his chest, and put a hydrating mask over his face for him to breathe. He had chest X-rays, sometimes three in one day, to check on the swelling caused by the pneumonia. By the weekend his lungs were mostly clear of congestion, and he had stopped coughing up phlegm and food.

Every other day, I went to the Claremont. After my workout, the moment I'd succumb to the shower's warmth, I'd think I'd hear my name called by club staff to tell me to return to the hospital. I'd turn off the shower and find no one there. I'd have the same moment of fright in the locker room when I'd check for phone messages. When I was ready to leave, I'd call Bob. "I'm fine," he'd say, "and looking forward to hearing about your adventures."

We curled together on the bed for afternoon naps and, in the evenings, watched TV. Once, after I'd read to Bob, he felt strong enough to read to me, which he did, until coughing overtook him. We had read to each other in the earlier years of our marriage, and now we had that pleasure again. Out the window, across the street, behind one of the rehabilitation houses, two trees were rooted so closely together their branches seemed to embrace. We often watched them, leaning together, supporting each other, rocking in the wind. We invested them with personality and gender, the larger male, the more delicate female. We adopted them as alter egos and relished their persisting.

My brother called. Two cousins sent cards. I heard from friends I'd made in elementary school and high school, summer camp and college, and served with in VISTA. Even "Miss Griffiths" (now Rev. Beamon), a favorite grade school teacher with whom I'd reconnected a few years earlier sent me a note. A lawyer-pal, who'd heard my office message, phoned. "Dude, you sounded awful. What happened?"

"I sounded 'awful'?" I said, thinking that might placate clients learning of my unavailability. "Good."

Friendships were important to me. It seemed that, once my sister's death had wrapped my parents in depression, I had sought pleasure outside the house with and through them. Unlike Adele, who kept in touch with virtually no one from her past, I had always responded to greeting cards, phone calls, and e-mails.

Most of these relationships remained perfunctory; many had ended abruptly or lain dormant for long periods, as events in other peoples' lives came to occupy them. Occasionally, though, the relationships had deepened in significance. The most surprising had been with Peter Cochrane, the wingback on the undefeated high school football team on which I had barely dirtied my uniform. After of a brief conversation at our fiftieth reunion, in which we'd exchanged references to our stints in therapy, we'd become correspondents. A real estate developer in Phoenix, Corky led a faith-based life – and sported an American flag lapel pin. ("Uh-oh," I had thought on first sighting.) Now he told me of his own heart attack and offered counsel. "Tell yourself," he said, "'I am blessed; I am healing; I am joyful; I am loved.'" Once I would have quickly struck the "Delete" button in my mind. Now, I began whispering his words to myself.

Though I did substitute "lucky" for "blessed."

I felt too crappy for visitors, but, utilizing his privileges as a physician, Budd stopped by. He had just lost, to esophageal cancer, an obstetrician friend, a daily swimmer at our club, the deliverer of his granddaughter, a lovely fellow – and younger than us both. Before Budd left, he kissed me.

All this caring moved me. I had rarely behaved like that. When someone was ill, I said the appropriate words; but I thought, "It is not me; it is not Adele." I shed no tears. I kissed no one. Now obits of strangers in the *Times* punched into me, like nails, for the pain in others their passings signified.

I felt myself a terrible person. I promised to do better.

As I kept Bob's friends in the loop through e-mail and phone, I thought about how different we were in this respect. I wasn't sure why I hadn't kept contact with people from my past. There had been unforgettable companions on each road I'd taken, but they remained where we'd left off, for their reasons or mine. Each ending formed a locus of great interest to me, which I often mined in my fiction writing. Maybe each move I made, from school to school, or city to city, seemed so cataclysmic, so full of the promise of arriving somewhere as if born anew, free of past definition, that I hoped to maximize the feeling that I could start over and be anyone I wanted.

Bob was the exception. With him I had experienced a continuity of development, his, mine, and our coupledom, and such a strong bond that it seemed, via fantasy, to go back into time before we met. He had loved me for who I was, not who I might or should become, and had given me the freedom and support to grow stronger in ways I'd felt broken. I hadn't thought we could feel/be any closer, but the past months had proved me wrong. Since his health crisis, I'd felt our love and trust and appreciation deepen.

My family was also a focus, whose support I counted on and from which I drew stability. My brother called twice a day. His son and daughter called too. My sister preferred I call her when I wished to talk, but we e-mailed almost daily. At Bob's urging I took most calls outside the room. He didn't want to hear me recite the ups and downs of the day, and this granted me the freedom to express my worries without being concerned how they might affect him.

Both Gordie and Sylvie offered to come out, but I said," Not now." I wanted to be alone with Bob as much as possible. It felt good to have an "away team" and a "home team" of friends who had offered help when we left Sutter.

One night, having my usual trouble falling asleep, even with a sleeping pill, I listened to patient call buttons, nurses' footsteps, telephones ringing, and, in our room, the buzz and click of the machinery. My first welcome steps toward sleep had begun when a Code Blue exploded. Loud speakers shrieked and a cart clattered up the hall. Those bells had rung for Bob while I stood helplessly outside the operating room. I had taken comfort in each day that passed without their awful sound. Now it shot adrenalin through my body, and I relived that panic.

I got out of bed, zipped up my purple hoodie, and wandered from the room. The halls of the ward formed a horseshoe, and the room with the patient in trouble was across the way. The door was open, and I could see him being worked on. Earlier in the evening, as Bob and I had strolled the corridors, that man – gray-haired, clad in a plaid bathrobe – now in need of resuscitation, had sat in a chair, talking with his middle-aged son. I walked up and down the hall, hoping the man would survive. I checked on Bob each time I passed our room. He was breathing easily, well asleep.

After twenty minutes, the cart was removed. A gurney took the man away. The door was closed and the room sealed off with yellow tape. I heard a nurse leave a message for the son. He would need to arrange to have the body picked up from the morgue. She saw me listening. "Are you having trouble sleeping?"

I said I was. "Could I make myself an herbal tea?"

She said I could. "How is your husband?"

After I told her, she said we were lucky. "My brother-in-law had the same kind of damaged heart. He lived two years, and my sister was grateful she had the time to prepare for life without him."

The tea helped. The promise of two years did not. I returned to our room, took a tranquilizer, and cried myself to sleep, adding the man's death and the nurse's tale to what I buried.

By my second week in Summit, I could go twenty-four hours without periods of total despair.

One morning Dr. Fleur visited. She brought, in Adele's words, "Strong light and deep hope" into the room. She was the angel that glowed the brightest. We believed that she would guide us toward the best that could be found.

An echo-cardiogram had showed my heart's ejection fraction, which measures the percentage of blood that pumps out with each beat, was forty-six percent, several points higher than when I'd lain in surgery. This was encouraging. "If you ask somebody who doesn't do heart failure," Dr. Fleur explained, "Fifty-five means a healthy heart. Heart-failure people, like me, anything over forty-five is good enough that you don't expect anything bad to happen from the heart. Thirty-five means trouble. And once the fluids are out of your system, you might be higher."

She re-assured me that I had not done myself in by over-exerting at rehab. I had turned out to be among the small percentage of people who are resistant to the blood-thinner Plavix, a failing for which there is no test. The result was I had thrown clots, which had blocked major arteries. "You are lucky it happened at rehab. If you had been driving home, you might not have made it."

Dr. Fleur had now placed me on Effient, a Plavix alternative, which had been developed two or three years earlier. She radiated confidence. But I wondered how I could have faith in this drug, given the unlikelihoods that had happened to me already? I was not supposed to have one heart attack; now I was on my second. "It can't work for all people," I said.

"Perhaps. But you would be the first for whom it didn't. You *must* believe you will live. We will return you to things you loved. Ten years ago, you would have died. Five years ago, you would have. Developments

54

occur daily. So you must stay positive. That you have survived two major heart attacks may mean God has something substantial in store for you."

That night I wet my bed.

I had dreamt I was engrossed in a virtual reality game, in which players competed for love, honor, and friendship. When players failed, the game provided no way for them to express disappointment. Was my urine, I wondered, my grief pouring out?

Adele had remarked that day that we had never been unlucky. We had assumed we would continue on that way, certainly without me being the first tripped by fate. Now we had to handle foreign terrain. "Fortunately," she'd said, "we did not depend on climbing mountains or running marathons for pleasure. We will not face adjustments of that magnitude."

By the following night, I was thinking how lucky I had been. I was off oxygen. I had circled the wing on my walker. I had made it the bathroom unassisted and shat. With a nurse's help, I had washed my face and front. I had even regained attitude. When the physical therapist told me my next step was a rehabilitation facility, I said, "No. I will be strong enough to go home."

About this time I had my first WOW realization. I had no magic! The awareness brought sadness, then relief. I could not keep Bob or myself well. I could only do my best to. I might wish I could control all variables, but magical thinking only set you up to experience guilt and inadequacy. I'd long thought I could make good or bad happen. When things didn't work out, I'd make myself try harder. But realizing the truth brought some relaxation and diminished guilt for earlier disasters. My mother's illnesses. All the people I had loved who'd died.

Like most new ground, it would need tending. But I felt safer and sturdier inside myself. I was sure it would be a back-and-forth swing for the rest of my life, but it seemed I had hit a psychological jackpot.

Before they would discharge me, I had to climb a flight of stairs. With my walker, I did. In my exuberance, I did a second.

When Dr. Fleur next visited, she brought good news – and bad. The good was that I could leave Summit the next day – and would not need a rehab center. "You need your own bed and the comforts of home," she said.

The bad came from the latest echo-cardiogram. The second M.I. had damaged my mitral valve. My heart was not properly expelling blood. I would, most likely, need surgery within thirty to sixty days. The operation would involve placing a ring around the valve to tighten it, like, as I understood it, replacing the washer to fix a leaky faucet.

Dr. Fleur assured us it was nothing major. "They enter through a small incision in your side. You are only hospitalized a few days."

I was reeling.

She would not discuss the risks of the procedure, or what repairs or maintenance the ring would require, or what future dangers I would face. "This is not the time or place. Summit has one of the best surgical units in the country. You will be in fine hands." The surgeon she had spoken to, Grover Doumanian, stopped by to introduce himself. He was stocky, silver-haired, almond-skinned. He was pleasant, assured, brisk. He sent his assistant to schedule an appointment for a consultation after my discharge.

My nurse was impressed. "When Dr. D's father needed a quadruple by-pass, he performed it. 'Why not?' he had said. 'My father is entitled to the best.'"

I was ready to separate from the hospital world and glad that Dr. Fleur supported the idea of our going home and complimented me, by saying she had every confidence the two of us would manage fine. Our bond with her seemed to strengthen each time she visited. I liked how she answered my frequent questions, and how she shared our pride in how far Bob had come. My confidence had grown too. I'd felt at home advocating for Bob and had enjoyed the nurses' appreciation of my efforts and that, in return, I'd made them feel good for all they'd done for him.

The night before Bob's discharge, the nurses turned off his machinery, so we'd get the feel of being unmonitored. In the morning, I did a preliminary pack of our belongings and made a couple trips with them to our car. Under the watchful eyes of one of our favorite nurses, Jodi, a smart and jazzy African-American woman, I solo changed the dressing on Bob's back. I scheduled our first home nursing visit and happily informed Social Services we would not need a rehab placement. I arranged for Robert to transport the bags I couldn't carry and for Marilyn and Griff to meet us at our house and help us settle. We took a last look at our two trees. They stood proud and strong, and we silently wished them good-bye.

After lunch, I brought the car to the front of the hospital. I was excited and nervous and clipped the driver's side door as I pulled up to pay the parking fee in the garage. It seemed right the Honda would be marked too. Bob stood up from the wheel chair and an attendant helped him into the passenger side. "Stay out of here," the attendant said.

I secured Bob's seat belt.

We both smiled, though tears were close too.

"Right?" I said at the corner.

"Left," Bob said.

It was strange to see people up and about, without pitchforks in their heads or scalpels in their futures. I determined to do all I could to rejoin them. Climbing the front stairs to our house was a challenge.

But once inside, I put the walker away and never used it again.

VIII. ANOTHER CHEST TO SAW THROUGH

Our bed is in the living room, under a cathedral ceiling and dark wood rafters. It is the nicest room in the house. We moved our bed there one rainy night in the '70s, when the bedroom flooded; and we stayed, once we realized our parents lived 3000 miles away and couldn't order us to return where we belonged. A playfully bobbing mobile dances above us and guards our dreams. Through the branches of our redwood and over the top of an orange-flowering eucalyptus, we see the smashing, ever-changing views of San Francisco and its bridges. Sometimes after dark, the city looks like a huge jewelry box; other times it hulks like a monster shrouded in fog.

Our walls are decorated with a Chagall lithograph, a piece of Robert's glass art, tiny objects collected over the decades, my own paintings, bright gobs of framed-and-hung inspiration: jazz ensembles; ski slopes; the state of Wyoming. Our shelves house hundreds of books, Samuel Beckett to Elmore Leonard, Joan Didion to Virginia Woolf. From our bed, holding hands while Bob tried to nap, I stared at the walls. I was on and off the bed a dozen times that first day. I arranged his pills, found the blood pressure machine, brought him applesauce, emptied his urine bottle, and unpacked.

When I called Sutter with a question about the medication plan, it took longer to get an answer than when we'd been there. The last days in the hospital now seemed a luxury cruise, with meals and laundry and pills taken care of. Bob had exceeded staff expectations, his determination and grit aiding recovery. He'd moved about the halls with increasing confidence. But on the home terrain, it felt like we were starting over, Bob's memories of how strong he'd once been and my images of life before the heart attacks rubbing against the reality of now.

We were too tired to confront a shower, but I provided a sponge bath and changed the dressing on Bob's back.

I had been in Summit sixteen days.

Now, washing my face and brushing my teeth, back-to-back, exhausted me. (There was no chance I could complete the trifecta and shave.) I was

58

taking twenty pills a day. The slightest irritant still triggered uncontrolled coughing. My pulse, which, when I had been healthy, had beat a steady sixty, clocked ninety. If I stood up too quickly, I became dizzy and risked falling. I could walk, at most, ten minutes, leaning on my cane, up and down the hall, in and out of rooms. I could not sleep or nap without a sleeping pill, or tranquilizer, or both; and when I slept, I'd wake after an hour or two and lie there, as if I had forgotten the rest of the steps to rising. I had lost fifteen-pounds. I imagined the men in the locker room would ask what gulag I had escaped from.

I was busier than I'd ever been in my life, including the semester I struggled through bio-chemistry without a background in basic or organic. (At least that I'd been allowed to take pass/fail.)

The tasks-to-do lined up from waking to sleep. And my sleep, except for the first two hours, when my need for it was stronger than anything, remained sporadic. I awakened when Bob coughed, trying not to worry it would upset his heart, or when he needed to go to the bathroom, trying not to worry he would fall, or on my own to find him anxiously waiting for enough time to have passed for him to take another sleeping pill.

During the day, as I went about preparing a meal, remaking the bed, retrieving the newspaper from wherever the carrier tossed it, cleaning, disinfecting and wrapping the wound from Bob's burst cyst, taking his blood pressure, helping him change clothes, calling drugstores for medication refills, washing dishes, doing laundries, planning future meals, and making lists for the grocery store, my mind would break each chore into component parts, smaller and smaller, to help me focus, until, sometimes, my brain felt it would burst. Mistakes occurred, or I injured myself when I raced past the tiny step at hand, or had a fantasy connected to the chore, or remembered something else I needed to do, stopping myself abruptly in whiplash fashion as I tried to go in two directions at once.

The hardest task was the shower. Bob became chilled so easily, I would first stoke up the heat in the bathroom. Then, dressed in a raincoat and shower cap to protect myself from becoming soaked, I would wash him as he sat in the tub on a plastic chair I'd purchased at a medical supply store. The water would bounce off the chair and me and over the curtain and soak the floor. By the time I had Bob wrapped in towels and the floor mopped up, I would have another load of laundry to do, grateful once again to Bob's mother for convincing me fifteen years earlier that accepting her gift of a washer-dryer would not brand Bob and me as irredeemably middle class bourgeoisie.

There were welcome periods of waking repose though, lying in bed with Bob, watching a favorite show or movie, feeling and expressing to each other the wonder we felt underneath the fears, struggles and uncertainties. Those moments sustained me.

The visiting physical therapist assigned me a half-dozen exercises to perform twice a day and provided a hand-out, "Yoga for the Heart." I performed weightless curls. I lifted one leg at a time. I followed my breath. The occupational therapist suggested I wash a few dishes and prepare portions of a meal to assist my conditioning. I did all Adele allowed me. A nurse checked my vital signs – and terrified us with warnings about potentially lethal blood clots lying in wait in my legs.

We took my blood pressure morning and evening. (I averaged 90/64, each low reading landing like a hammer on a toe.) I weighed myself daily, and if I had gained two-pounds within twenty-four hours, I had to take a potassium-loaded medication to induce more frequent urination. It tasted awful and made me choke and cough. To protect against swelling in the lower legs and those lethal clots, I wore support socks, which I could not put on without Adele's assistance. I kept tissue, bottled water, and my cell phone on a table beside the bed to reduce how often I had to leave it. My back still rested against my plastic "doughnut," positioned so the cyst wound would not further inflame. I peed in a bottle. If I banged any portion of my body, I bled.

Adele would not leave home to shop or exercise unless a friend babysat me. ("Bobsat," Adele called it.) Marilyn came when not teaching. Robert practiced his shakuhachi while I rested or walked. Budd, Artie, others came too. It all helped. When these friends sought assurances I was doing well, not wishing to disappoint, I said, "Sure"; but I believed myself, oh, two or three percent recovered. If someone tried to share a personal problem with me, a misbehaving son, an unsatisfying relationship, I was overwhelmed, lacking the emotional capacity to deal with anyone's troubles but my own.

That first week, I went out only to have our dermatologist assess whether the cyst site had become infected, which would have meant postponement of my surgery. Entering her building, I felt as frail as any of the walker-clutching, wheelchair-mounted, or oxygen-toting others. Dr. Allasandro said the cyst would have healed no better if treated by a professional. That made Adele feel good but led me to say, after we'd left, that I feared, should the need arise, I could never provide her equivalent care.

"You'll get help," Adele said. "Or maybe you won't have to. And we'll always have Switzerland."

She meant a clinic in Geneva which performed assisted suicides. When we'd learned of it, a year earlier, we had joked we would acquire one-way tickets to keep with us at all times, like settlers saving the last bullet in case of Apaches.

I decided I owed her my best effort to recover. All the cases I'd handled in my law practice of lives disrupted by snapped scaffolding or overturned backhoes, improperly lifted lumber or too frequently manipulated keyboards had taught me I had no ultimate control over my course's outcome. No one ever did. Any day you woke, you were not guaranteed to see evening. But you could do all you could to make it happen.

Slowly, things improved.

I became less dependent on sleeping pills. My in-house walks now included a trip down and up our back stairs. I read my first book (Kate Atkinson's *Case Histories*). I sat in a chair for two consecutive hours. I ate most meals seated at the dining room table. I raised my estimated percentage of recovery to five percent. I did not know if that was the

Lexapro or an innate human capacity to adjust and carry on, as though the fragility of existence was not a consideration.

Still I felt I could not get anywhere until the operation. And counting on an operation seemed a bet against great odds.

Bob handled the visits from the ever-changing nurses and therapists better than I did. I hated the I-pads they filled by asking the same questions of us, rather than passing the information to each other. I hated the repeated warnings about what could go wrong. I hated the worried questions each visit summoned from me to have answered.

Having to weigh Bob daily revived an old, uncomfortable obsession about my own weight. Plus, a depression, whose grip I had escaped, was creeping back. It had arisen two years before, when I had been unable to find an agent for a memoir I'd written about my relationship to tennis. This had coincided with the early days of the home repair that became the subject of Mold Central. *Originally estimated as taking six weeks, the work was still unfinished. Our contractor had discovered more and more dry rot and had been bedeviled by incompetent workers, licensing snafus and his own poor health and bad planning. Bob had delayed his retirement to earn the money it cost, and I'd felt guilty about my short work history, which had made our finances tight. I'd even had months of terror obsessing that my own heart was failing, but, after testing, these fears were diagnosed as part of the depression.*

Bob's heart attacks had left me fully alert to each moment, occupied by his care. During the day, I felt buoyed by Bob's presence, our closeness, and the importance of all I could do to aid his recovery. But during my insomniac nights, the depression and worries returned. I would not take sleeping pills because I feared not waking if Bob needed me and because I hated the groggy state of the next day. I preferred the exhaustion.

My second Monday home, Adele and I saw Dr. Fleur. She continued to exude confidence and, stressing the crucial role the brain played in the healing process, emphasized the importance of my feeling positive. We turned to her like plants the sun. We appreciated that she registered our closeness. She praised Adele for having stood up to everything she had faced without crumbling. "Elle est votre ame," Dr. Fleur said. "How lucky you are to have each other."

She eliminated two medications, reduced the dosage of others, added a tranquilizer and two diuretics to decrease fluid retention – and doubled my Lexapro. She said my weight loss – now 12 pounds – was fine. "The surgeon will be pleased. He won't be slicing through fat. 'I know there's a heart in here somewhere...'"

She also said an operation might prove unnecessary. By adjusting my medications, she might coax my valve into behaving. In any event, I should not be swayed by anything Dr. Doumanian said. He was not, she warned, known for his bedside manner. "To a hammer, everything's a nail."

I would hear that expression a few times over the next days.

Our appointment was for 9:00. He saw us at 11:30. That allowed ample time to study the plaques and certificates on his waiting room wall.

The first thing Dr. Doumanian said was that four percent of valve repair patients died during surgery. Six percent, he went on, suffered kidney failure, or liver failure, or pulmonary embolisms, or double pneumonia, or a stroke, or excessive bleeding, which they survived but which might require six months hospitalization. Then he said my stents made impossible the minimal invasion Dr. Fleur had mentioned. He would need to open my chest, which meant more risk, a longer hospitalization, and lengthier recovery. But if I did not have surgery, I might not live five years. To reduce the chance of my suffering a third – and fatal – M.I., the sooner I had the operation the better. Each sentence pressed upon me like an inquisitor's stone set on a heretic's chest. Chests seemed to come without thoughts or emotions to Dr. Doumanian. I was, I felt, another one to saw through.

He opened his appointment book.

"But Dr. Fleur said I might not need surgery."

"You are my patient now. You will have it when I say."

His first opening was in three weeks. He wrote my name on the line.

IX. THE RETURN OF
MR. MIRACLEMAN

The visit to Dr. Doumanian left me feeling like I imagined Wile E. Coyote did, after the steamroller flattened him. But when I called Dr. Fleur, she said, "Forget everything he told you. He overstepped his bounds. I had only mentioned I might have a patient for him, and he bulled his way in. My job is to decide if and when you have surgery. Yours is to grow stronger and feel better."

When I called Dr. Doumanian's office to cancel the surgery, his secretary said he would check with Dr. Fleur to be certain that was what she wanted. Until the scheduled date of the operation had passed, I feared he would convince her to change her mind. Even when it had passed, I wondered if I could live comfortably, knowing what he'd told me.

Well, you had to hear the statistics sometime, I told myself. Now you have longer to process them.

The threat of surgery hung over us. We could beat it back, but it never disappeared. Dr. Zipp, Bob's PCP, encouraged the idea that he could simply accept his present condition and refuse the operation. It felt good to hear we had the choice, but we knew we would do whatever Dr. Fleur recommended, even if it meant going ahead with Dr. Doumanian. I had taken a violent dislike to him. His imperious manner went well beyond that of any surgeon I had before encountered, but I believed she would best safeguard Bob's life.

The third session with the physical therapist, I walked, cane-in-hand, twenty feet down the hill on which our house sits, to the corner and back. "Congratulations," she said, "you've graduated."

The next day, with Adele beside me, I walked for ten minutes on flat ground. I had to consider whether to step off each curb and continue for another block. Scaling the slightest incline set me breathing hard. The cold air brought a nasal drip that set me coughing. I was exhausted by the time we'd returned to the car; but the next day I did sixteen minutes – and the day after that, twenty.

Through April, May and June, I made other gains. When Adele and I read to each other, my portions grew longer and louder. I exercised at the club with two-pound weights and, afterwards, lay in the sun. My arms toned, and my color brightened. My mood brightened too. I met friends at cafes and occasionally accompanied my espresso with a self-indulgent mini-cannoli. I replaced my cane with a silver-handled, bone-tipped, ebony walking stick Adele had bought me as a gift in the flamboyant '60s.

But I still needed pills to sleep. My coughing and dizziness remained. I continued to bruise and bleed easily. My weight kept falling – 163, 161, 158. My systolic blood pressure, which measures the pressure in the arteries when the heart beats, hung in the high eighties or low nineties. Surgery seemed to draw closer with each reading. I planned to update my will.

You survived two heart attacks falling upon you from the blue, I reminded myself. You should survive a pre-planned operation, surrounded by an entire hospital. With this view in place, I accessed pleasure in unaccustomed places. Conversations at the French, about the CIA being behind 9-11, which intruded into my efforts to read or write, did not cause me to seek a quieter – and saner – corner. Waiting in check-out lines behind customers who ran back for broccoli or chatted with the cashier about skiing conditions in the Sierras did not drive me into mutterings or foot-taps.

I was happy to be there. I was happy to be.

Dr. Fleur complimented my improved mood and increased activities. My lungs were clear and my blood work fine. My heart beat steadily and, though she could detect a murmur, it was doing "all that is asked of it." My BNP (Brain Natriuretic Peptide), a hormone produced to make the kidney pee more, when the amount of fluid in the cardiovascular system is too high, which had been 2000 when I was in Summit, was now 600. ("*Yes!*"

Dr. Fleur exclaimed when she saw it.) When my blood pressure registered 101 in her presence, she joked I'd become "hypertensive."

We would not rush toward surgery. She wished to allow my medications more time to work – and Summit additional time to approve use of a newly developed device that could keep me alive if my heart failed during the operation. She also wanted me to re-enter cardiac rehabilitation.

I balked. I could not forget my last effort had ended with me puking on a bench, wheeled out on a gurney. Each step I took forward seemed to expose a deeper, more threatening pit to view.

But two weeks later, after having walked for thirty consecutive minutes, I said, "Okay." (This was more confidence than I had shown about swimming. Since my first M.I., I had felt I belonged on land and had not re-entered the pool.) I could not deny my progress, though I had not extinguished my concerns. Once I had believed I would live into my eighties, no problem, and maybe my nineties. Now I worried I would not last long enough to learn who had murdered Rosie in *The Killing*.

When I mentioned to Robert, during a walk in Tilden Park, that I often consciously brought to mind all I'd been through, he asked why. His father had been so overwhelmed by his heart attack that he had basically withdrawn from life.

"It focuses me," I said, "on how far I've come."

Adele drove me to and from my first rehab session – and every one thereafter. She had not forgiven herself for not being there for my second heart attack. It did not matter that I said her presence would have not affected what happened. Or that she may have driven me to Alta Bates, instead of Summit, where the outcome might have been different.

"Mr. Miracleman," a nurse greeted me.

"So you've got the full jacket," another said, having read in my chart of my number of stents.

The staff babied me. I was not permitted to exercise with more than one-pound weights. The settings on my cardio-machines were set at new lows. But things gradually grew more challenging – and I met the challenges.

One morning, while on the treadmill, I saw my father staring back from the mirror before me. The bald head. The glasses. The twinkle in the eye.

My father had been my difficult parent. A scrappy South Philly kid, he'd become a lawyer, Democratic ward leader in down-and-dirty big city politics, later a judge. He had set the standards I felt I had to meet. It had taken Adele to convince me of his essential sweetness – and how his outward manner came from his own insecurities. I still had the last birthday card he sent me, a few months before bladder cancer claimed him. It showed a smiling puppy with a heart-shaped balloon tied to its tail. The inside said, "May good things follow wherever you go."

It was nice to see my Dad. I regretted all the man-to-man talks we had never had. But I was not ready to pull up a cloud across from him and sit down for a face-to-face.

The cardio-rehab schedule took getting used to, but it also anchored the week and made the days off feel spacious and precious and full of choices.

While Bob was at his sessions, I'd take walks. As I'd exit, I'd feel a burst of energy and often sang, but as soon as I heard an emergency vehicle's siren and saw flashing lights heading toward where I'd been, I would hurry back to make sure Bob was okay. I'd see him on a bike or treadmill, smile, and walk out the door again. Once, though, the para-medics beat me to the rehab center, and my mind screamed, "This is it!"

But it was for another poor fellow.

When we next saw Dr. Fleur, she greeted us, "My favorite couple."

She dismissed the black-and-blue marks which dotted my body as nothing to worry about. Neither was my blood pressure, which remained low, even after exercise. That, she explained, was natural, given the medications I was on. As long as I did not feel dizzy when I walked, it was fine. The best news was her inability to "feel" my heart on physical examination. That meant, she said, with amazement in her voice, that the swelling had reduced even further.

Then we discussed food. A consulting dietician at rehab had recommended I gain weight by, for instance, adding bagels spread with peanut butter to my menu. Dr. Fleur said to ignore her. While she would not mind me heavier, say, 165, my present weight was fine. And sodium, with which bagels were loaded, because of its effect on blood pressure was my "enemy."

So there went pretzels and pastrami and pickles. And Chinese and Mexican and Thai food. There went, in fact, almost any restaurant, and all canned foods, and most breads. I envisioned a life sustained by root vegetables and nuts.

But I would bite this bullet too.

"Be sensible, though," Dr. Fleur said, "not punitive." She turned to Adele. "Keep him bubbly."

I would have an echo-cardiogram in six weeks. Even if it showed surgery was necessary, I was in such good condition, I would not be at risk.

Adele and I left, reassured. I felt I might be entering the next phase of life. But I wondered again who I would be, with even pastrami subtracted from me.

Two days later, heavy coughing set my heart beating 136 times a minute, and we were back at Dr. Fleur's. When her massage of my carotid artery did not correct the misfire, she scheduled me for an electric shock – fifty joules – two hours later. "I have done a million," she said, "and no one has ever died."

It was over so quickly, I was returned to the holding room without remembering having left it. I thought of my good fortune compared to those who lay around me in their cubicles awaiting more drastic procedures.

I knew tachycardia was a bad sign. I sat in the waiting room, while the shock was administered. I was as nervous as if it was life-threatening. I carried a beeper, which the hospital provided next-of-kin, so I could be summoned if I went to the bathroom, or the cafeteria, or across the street to the grocery.

I watched so many others get buzzed that, unable to wait any longer, I had the clerk at the reception desk inquire if Bob was done. The clerk said he had returned from surgery, was awake and receiving fluids to raise his blood pressure. I waited ten more minutes, then went downstairs and convinced a nurse to let me sit with Bob. Only when I saw him did I calm down.

I had been wound up tight for weeks. My feet hurt. I needed a haircut. I needed an orgasm. I was due a teeth-cleaning, a glaucoma check, my annual whole-body skin check, and a physical. I had lost weight. I spent a lot of time alone in my head. I couldn't unburden myself by crying without a weak vein in my nose bursting, unleashing a torrent of blood, leaving me weak. My solution was to hold back the tears, which felt inhuman, since I wanted to cry almost every day.

I needed to unburden myself to Bob and be comforted by him, but I feared over-burdening him. I e-mailed my worries to my sister and Marilyn, which took off some pressure. My brother's daily calls provided further relief. Finally I told Bob I felt the need to focus on my own life but also feared that, if he had surgery, I wouldn't be able to care for him.

He didn't crumble. We continued to talk. I felt better and found the energy to write some.

I returned to rehab the day following my "shock." But my weight had jumped three-and-a-half-pounds in twenty-four hours and Adele – and the nurses – were concerned.

It was back to Dr. Fleur. She was surprised to see us – but not unpleased. When my lungs and blood pressure and the results of an EKG all showed me to be fine, she sent us on our way. "That woman!" she said, admiring Adele's attentiveness. "Take her to a show."

I smiled – but recognized how quickly things could turn.

As if to underline this, a phone message from Budd was waiting when we got home. Headaches, which his ophthalmologist had passed off as routine, had turned out to be a brain tumor.

"If you have to have one," he said, "mine is the best kind."

"And just after our first kiss," I said.

After completing thirty days of participation, the cardio-rehab staff gives you a pedometer. I accepted mine as gratefully as if it was a Phi Beta Kappa key.

My cyst had healed. I'd resumed meditating. My blood pressure once reached 112. I read an entire history of the Freedom Riders. I wrote an account of my heart attacks for *The Broad Street Review*, an on-line journal to which I regularly contributed, the effort suggesting to me I had found closure with them. We bought a flat screen TV, an indulgence to which we felt eminently entitled. Life was fine. Then, during a rehab session, my heart rate, which had been as low as forty-five beats-per-minute two days before, hit 154.

This time Dr. Fleur prescribed two medications, Amiodarone and Warfarin, and anticipated my beginning Coumadin, which required patients to give blood twice a week, so its effects could be monitored and its dosage adjusted. Even more gloomily, her assessment was that the rapid heartbeat, combined with my continued low blood pressure, increased surgery's likelihood.

I felt mad – as well as worried. I had been ready for a run of good feelings." Will we ever feel good again?" I asked Adele.

"In a couple days," she said. "But I admit I hadn't planned to spend our Golden Years like this."

"I certainly thought we'd eat out more," I said.

The next day, my heart stayed in rhythm through an entire rehab session.

And Dr. Fleur called. She had reviewed my records and decided I didn't need Coumadin after all. Avoiding those bleedings was as big a lift as hitting three gold bars on a Vegas slot machine. All my readings returned to previous levels – and my heart beat as regularly as if Papa Jo Jones was working it.

My feelings and activity level improved. But the better I functioned, the more I felt the depression pressing underneath. My dreams were full of it but vanished before I could work with them. I didn't have the energy to seek psychiatric help, and I was too frightened to try an anti-depressant. My sense of identity wobbled as my writing ceased again. I had always been able to use it to process what was happening to me, no matter how sad or grim. I would hear my voice offering sentences or composing scenes which worked things through, entertaining myself on walks, before sleep, or while swimming. Now I found nothing in the present for the future.

The days slipped by, my only company things-to-do or worries-to-tame. The fun part of my mind was empty. I could have fun with Bob, but I wondered what had happened to the rest of me. Was it part of aging? Was a sick husband just beyond such management? Was my mix of internal and external terrors too much to cope with? I was gainfully employed caring for Bob, but when he was better, what would happen to me?

I passed the number of rehab sessions I'd had when my second M.I. had occurred. I passed the number of weeks on Effient that I'd been on Plavix when I'd clotted. On August 2, Adele and I celebrated our fortieth anniversary. My confidence rose.

And dipped. Some nights I needed two tranquilizers and two sleeping pills. After Adele reported my ankles appeared swollen, Dr. Galloway, who was covering me while Dr. Fleur was on vacation, doubled my Lasix. When my morning pulse hit a new low, Estelle, the office nurse-assistant, halved my Amiodarone. When Dr. Zipp blamed it for an abnormal liver function, which had registered on a blood panel he'd ordered, I wondered if it was the cause of all my problems, low blood pressure, dizziness, weight loss, even my baldness.

That I could joke seemed a good sign. But I wasn't about to stop a medication until Dr. Fleur agreed.

Which she did.

A week or so after his surgery, I visited Budd. We sat in his backyard while a ruby-throated hummingbird sampled the honeysuckle. Each of us kept in our studies a snapshot of six boys who had played softball together, the summer of 1949, in Beach Haven, New Jersey. Neither of us recognized anyone in the picture now, except each other. We could name the pennant-winning Whiz Kids of 1950 though. Eddie Waitkus, Granny Hamner, Puddin' Head Jones. Their names passed through our lips like rosary beads through fingers. As time stripped people, places, things from you, all you could hold onto seemed a jewel to pocket.

"I could live at this level of function," I said. "In fact, I feel like the luckiest guy in the world."

He said he was.

It was not a bad competition to be part of.

X. THE LAMB CHOP

The results of the echo-cardiogram landed August 25th. Adele and I expected to hear, "Things are improving."

Dr. Fleur said, "The medications have done all they can."

There was good news and bad – and the good didn't matter. I felt fine; I enjoyed cardio-rehab; I had regained a couple pounds. My ejection fraction had climbed to 46.4, which ranked me, she said, "Among the kings of my practice." But part of my heart was not working. It did not pump sufficient blood. I had, it seemed, a "severely dilated left atrium," "severe mitral regurgitation and atrial arrhythmia." I needed to proceed to surgery.

"You are thin and fit," Dr. Fleur said. "Your other organs are fine. You have a ninety-nine percent chance of coming through the operation. And if your heart fails, devices will be available to save you."

I had recently set personal bests on two machines at rehab. It had not prevented me from noting that same evening Wallace Stegner's remark, in *Crossing to Safety*, "Survival, it is called… always it is temporary." I am blessed, I thought. I am healing…

"Believe me, I have given my recommendation much thought. I will select a surgeon and hospital as if I am choosing them for myself."

It was hard seeing Bob thrown by the news, but he adjusted to this new reality, which helped me get there too. He quickly accepted that the operation was his chance to get even better, while, at first, I'd clung to impossibilities, even wasted energy with fantasies, like, if it had been done when Dr. Doumanian suggested, Bob would already have recovered. But I knew that fighting reality made it harder to access Dr. Fleur's reassurances and my own hopes for an improved life for Bob and for us. When I became able to give up my fantasies, Bob was relieved and happy at my leap. Being on the same page strengthened both of us.

We promised each other to enjoy each day we had.

Three days later, Dr. Fleur called to announce her choices. The hospital was California Pacific, on the outskirts of the Pacific Heights neighborhood, in San Francisco. It possessed equipment which could keep me alive, which Summit had not yet approved. Its chief surgeon, Vesuvio Volpe, had promised Dr. Fleur to operate himself, rather than pass me off to an assistant, and since she would be on vacation, its chief cardiologist, under whom she'd done her residency, had promised to attend me.

Oh, yes, I might need a valve replacement, not simply a ring.

And if I needed a transplant, they had promised I could have one.

The transplant was another "Where-did-that-come-from?" moments. I seemed to have gone from lean-and-mean to doddering-and-rotted in a minute.

My favorite cardio-rehab nurse reassured me with reports on the good results she had seen on Dr. Volpe's patients, but I remained wobbly, and Adele was reeling. She was sorry, for one thing, if the hospital had to be across the bay, it was not U.C. Med. Center, with whose neighborhood she was familiar and where, as an alumnus, she might be allowed use of the gym. I said we could probably find a nearby hotel with an exercise room. There was no way, I knew, she could leave me, drive herself home, and sleep.

I had my own physical. My doctor was empathetic to our situation, and I carried her reassuring certification of good health close to my heart. I also carried her prescriptions for a tranquilizer and sleeping pill, which I needed because Bob's cough kept me up nights; and, without sleep, I became more vulnerable and angry. The pills calmed me, stopped my fearful fantasies, and let me sleep.

I cooked us healthy meals. I helped a friend edit her husband's obituary. I distracted myself with the U.S. Open, noting my reaction to my long-time favorite Roger Federer's wins and losses had become more muted.

Roger was the player who had kicked my lifelong tennis fandom over the moon. I'd played tennis since my first summer of away camp, thirty-one years before he was born. It was the only sport I took to, winning the doubles for the

"Brown" team, though the youngest player by four years. I dreamed of becoming a pro. I idolized Vic Seixas, Little Mo, Pancho Gonzalez as others did movie stars. But it wasn't until Roger that I saw in a player everything I'd imagined and more. But now I had no energy for a fanatic's exuberance or extended days of mourning. Bob's coming through his operation, his recovery and then, if necessary, attending to my own, trumped any fandom. I'd once joked to Bob, "Roger is the only man I'd leave you for." Now it hurt to even think that.

Evenings we read Kate Atkinson's third detective novel to each other. I dreaded finishing it because we didn't have a replacement for the hospital. The natural choice was her fourth, which had just been published, but Bob's Law of Book Buying forbade purchase until we found a used copy.

Dr. Volpe had Dr. Doumanian's self-confidence but worn in a more comforting fashion. He was on time for our appointment and unrushed. Instead of leading with the risks I faced, he handed us a booklet, in which I could learn about them – or choose not to. When he slipped a five-percent fatality figure into the conversation, he repeated Dr. Fleur's assurance that my good condition meant I would do fine. When he learned Adele and I wrote, he said he had majored in English at Harvard and quoted Auden. When he learned that Dr. Fleur had considered Stanford for me, he claimed superiority to any surgeon there. He described the heart's workings with the zeal of an intern. He declared operations still enthralled him. When he said my valve would be replaced by a pig's, he tossed one to me, encased in plastic. While I wondered if its incorporation would disqualify me from minyans, he added he expected I would need two by-passes and "some tinkering with your electrical system."

"The operation will take three hours. You'll be in the hospital one week, and your recovery will take five. You'll feel like a Mack truck hit you. Then a car. Then a bicycle. You'll want to hibernate, withdraw, be left alone. But start moving; start building up; keep at it forever. The heart is a muscle. It likes that."

Dr. Volpe answered all my questions, including where I might stay. The hospital had an arrangement with the Kabuki, a hotel in Japantown, with special rates for relatives of patients and an hourly shuttle bus, to and fro. I booked myself in for a week.

Its on-line site made it look so grand, Bob and I promised each other we'd spend a weekend there for pleasure.

We were relieved the decision was made. We stopped taking my blood pressure. I stopped cardio-rehab two weeks short of completion. I would do this and begin again. I enjoyed each trip to the Claremont, each lunch out, each book store browsed. If a positive attitude affected a surgery's outcome, I would have one. I ordered a pair of Mark Nason boots from Neiman Marcus, demonstrating $175 worth of belief that I would survive to enjoy them.

My next walk with Robert was along Caesar Chavez Park, on the Berkeley waterfront. A strong, cold wind was in our face. I wondered if I would make it to the end.

The surgery was scheduled for September 29. I had moments of terror and moments of despair. I feared the waiting while they worked on Bob. I feared being unable to talk to him for days. If we were separated for five minutes, I wept.

"We handled it before," Bob said. "We'll handle it."

One afternoon, following a particularly bad night's sleep, I napped. When I woke, I told Bob it had felt safe, having him, awake and protective, beside me.

We got back into our routine. We knew the anxiety would crescendo again as the surgery approached. Each day seemed long and full and precious, slowed down.

Marilyn offered to be with me the day of the operation, for which I was grateful. Robert offered to drive us to the hospital, pick up our mail each day, and deposit it in a box in the garage, so he or Marilyn could deliver it when coming to visit. I duplicated house keys for each of them.

I purchased a tablet for e-mailing, tennis news, and other on-line distractions. I packed a bag with what I'd need for the week and re-filled prescriptions. We bought a commode and placed it a step away from the bed for when Bob returned from the hospital. His not having to trek to the toilet would help us both sleep through the night.

I took care of myself too. I had a skin check after a pimple I'd picked became infected. My dermatologist warned me if it didn't clear up, I'd need to conceal it, or I wouldn't be allowed near Bob in the hospital. That upset me more than hearing she needed to check it in a month, in case it needed to be biopsied. She gave me an antibiotic cream and, fortunately, the blemish vanished quickly. I also had a haircut, which turned out four inches shorter than I'd asked.

"How could you miss by so much?" I asked my stylist.

"You looked so tired and drawn," she said, "I thought it would make you feel better."

Meanwhile, the doctors discussed alternative approaches. Actually, they feuded.

Dr. Fleur said she had told Dr. Volpe to get in, fix my valve, and get out. "You don't need these other things," she explained. "They do them because they're money-makers, and they do them wrong, or they fix the wrong places. I want you out of the hospital ASAP."

But Dr. Volpe convinced her to allow him to do any by-passes I needed in order to avoid having to unzip me in the future. She remained adamant about the "tinkering" though, whose benefits were less assured. I felt like a lamb chop, with chefs debating my garnishing; but a new echo-, ordered to give Dr. Volpe a current view of my situation, was encouraging. A wall Dr. Fleur had believed dead had come alive from the medications. The surgery's potential gains now included a significantly increased life span.

"You're such an exciting case," Dr. Fleur said.

I overlooked Dr. Tao having said I should hope never having to hear anything like that said about me.

The week before the operation, Bob's review of William Boyd's Nat Tate: An American Artist *was published on-line. The book had been released and responded to as an actual biography; but Boyd had made everything up, not only the life events, but the journal entries, letter extracts, and recollections of friends.*

Bob had worked on his piece the preceding month. I didn't know how he could remain so focused or, conversely, why I had so little control in similar situations. Some years before, when a longstanding melanoma, hidden under bushels of my hair, had me facing surgeries and, depending on its stage of development, radiation or chemo — or death — I'd had visions worth describing but couldn't bring myself to write a word. (I'd had the surgery and surprised the doctors – and myself – with the best possible lab results: Stage One.) Perhaps, I thought, writing took Bob's mind off his operation by filling him with other thoughts. What filled me was watching thriller movies on cable, where the fears experienced by anonymous people were greater than my own.

Reading Bob's review, I wondered, too, if the subject matter, or his analysis of the situation, related to what was going on in his life. His recent medical events must have felt like they were happening to a person he hadn't expected to be, a fictional Bob, not the real Bob. The most striking thing about his reaction to the shocks he had survived was the positive way he had changed in order to manage them. He still felt like Bob to me, but there was more of him than previously. He was friendlier to himself and others, more empathic; and when he wrote, his mind reached for more than in the past. This was all good.

Dr. Fleur ordered an angiogram for me at Alta Bates to make sure the echo- had not registered a false positive. It seemed I was having a test a day and awaiting results and next steps in-between. That was probably always the case before surgeries and a good thing that doctors macro- and micro- focused to assure best outcomes, but it was nerve racking.

"I'm hoping," Adele said. "I need endorphins. I haven't had an *in*dorphin in days. I'm only having *out*dorphins."

It took two tranquilizers to put me to sleep the night before the test. A nurses' strike was threatened, and it was unclear if a tech would be available for me. If there wasn't, Dr. Volpe would have to postpone the operation. Even if there was, I would have to wait for the results. And, now that we knew there was an upside, they mattered greatly.

Because of the strike, Alta Bates seemed staffed by temps from another planet, where all motion was slowed down, and even the simplest tasks, like finding an extra blanket, was bewildering. It was not long before their hesitations and fumblings left us giggling each time they left our room.

It took six hours, but the test was done.

The echo- had been right. The wall lived. And the doctors discovered another place that they hadn't known about, which would benefit from additional blood flow as well.

I felt almost insanely good.

Before I had resented people who were heart-problem free, when I, who had lived right wasn't, and they, who hadn't, were. Now I saw myself as having an "opportunity." I would have an experience that they had not. I would be better physically than I had been. I would emerge deeper, wiser, stronger.

Adele said she had similar hopes but had been scared to express them. "Like your Arizona friend said about faith. Love and desire are stronger than fear."

Over our long weekend, we enjoyed our café time and workouts, and added a restaurant outing. At home, we ate our favorite meals, scallops and pasta, egg-white omelets, and hamburgers with olive oil home fries. We watched the always enchanting Bringing Up Baby *and the pricey same-day-as-in-theaters* Moneyball. *Family and friends called with best wishes. Marilyn and I worked out our plans for the day of the operation. Bob and I cuddled on the way to sleep.*

By Wednesday, it felt safe to jump into what I had dubbed "The-day-before-the-operation-will-be-over." I was pleased with how my mind had framed it. I find it hard to absorb both good news and bad news and come out with the positive, but it had been wonderful to hear Bob's thoughts about getting this done and having an improved life. I still had bad patches, but this second-hand smoke of good feelings prevailed most of the time.

Robert drove us to California Pacific. Since the '89 earthquake, I had been nervous crossing the Bay Bridge. I can't wait for Angel Island. Then I can't wait for the city. I was more nervous now.

We stopped at the Kabuki first. My room was lovely, but in hopes of staying overnight with Bob, I took a change of clothes and my pill box and tablet to the hospital in my backpack.

Once we were inside, it was BANG! BANG! BANG! Personal questions, temperature, pulse, blood pressure. Blood sample, urine. Physical exam, history, X-rays. It kept my mind off what was about to happen.

There were two beds in my room, and Adele was allowed to stay. The ward doctor, who was the last to visit, apologized for being late. He had wanted to read my substantial file before meeting with us. He was astounded at how well I looked, after all I'd been through. He discussed the operation and recovery time, leaving Adele and I feeling reassured.

We said our now-customary good nights, which end with "I feel loved."

The only bad omen was that, the next morning, the nurse shaving Bob, pre-op, nicked one of his testicles, and he bled and bled.

I held a towel and applied pressure to the spot. The amount of blood and the time it took to stop terrified me. After the bleeding stopped, Bob and I sat in the hall and people-watched. The call to surgery came shortly after noon, three hours later than expected. We were taken downstairs, where we met the anesthesiologist. We warned him about Bob's throat sensitivity, and he gave Bob something to relax him. I wished he'd medicate me too.

Bob and I parted with a kiss. It was not as hard to separate as after the second heart attack, when he felt and looked like he might not make it.

I am joyful. I have faith. I will be healed. I am loved.

XI. HAPPY OPERATION!

A grandmotherly woman, with short white hair and a nice smile, had me add my name, Bob's, his surgeon's, and my cell phone number to the list at the front desk. She showed me the board where I could see when Bob's surgery began, when it concluded, when he arrived in recovery, and when he was ready for his overnight in the ICU. His surgeon, she said, would visit me after completion. Marilyn was on her way. I felt safe, protected; my tranquilizer was kicking in.

Many people were already waiting, some reading newspapers, others on computers, a lone woman staring at a TV on the far wall, several sitting, eyes closed, perhaps asleep. I took two seats together for me and Marilyn, with a view outdoors and a small hassock we could share or use as a table. Then I returned to the desk for help with connecting to Wi-Fi. A young man fiddled with set-up and succeeded. Marilyn called from the garage, and I gave her directions to where I waited.

It was wonderful to feel her loving warmth. Everyone should be so lucky as to have a friend like her. Scrabble gave way to gin rummy, then to go-fish, as my attention span shortened.

At 1:30, a full hour before the expected finish, Dr. Volpe sat down with us. "A happy operation," he said. He had repaired Bob's mitral valve; a replacement hadn't been necessary. He'd only done one bypass. His assistant, Dr. Ivanov, and his team were closing. He suggested I go back to the hotel, relax, nap, eat something. I could see Bob in two hours in the ICU. I gave him a big hug and "Thank you."

I hugged Marilyn. I was shivering. I hugged myself. In two hours I could hug Bob. "Happy operation!" I said, trying out the words. "It's over. I'm so relieved."

Marilyn and I took the shuttle to the Kabuki. The clouds had cleared, the fog dispersed, the sea of terror calmed. I didn't want a nap or food, but I did want a shower and change of clothes. I'd never enjoyed a shower so thoroughly. I called my sister and brother and Bob's brother to tell them the good news. I convinced a reluctant-to-leave-me-alone Marilyn to cross the bay before the traffic built up.

I walked her to her car in the hospital garage and promised to call after I saw Bob. I took a leisurely walk around the block and arrived back at the time Dr. Volpe had suggested.

The board said Bob was still in surgery.

"Why?" I asked the grandmotherly woman.

She called the surgical nurse.

All she said was that they were working on Bob.

I called Dr. Volpe, but he was unreachable, in surgery at another hospital.

I was left to imagine the worst.

For the next four hours, I received periodic updates from the desk, each with the same, non-specific information.

I alternated pacing, sitting, and, eventually, curling in a fetal position, propped upon my backpack, on a bench. I kept my eye on the desk, having told them to wake me if I fell asleep and there was news. Joey, my niece in L.A., had received the "All clear" from her Dad and called me to rejoice. I told her what was going on, and we stayed in touch while I waited. That was a comfort, as was talking to Marilyn.

I was furious at Dr. Volpe's unavailability. His "Happy Operation" mockingly echoed in my ears. I told myself it might still be okay, but the possibility that it wouldn't rang full force. I worried that Bob had had a stroke or heart attack or was bleeding to death. I felt intolerable pain, psychic and physical, which alternated with numbness. I prayed I would not lose Bob. That was the abandonment I feared.

Finally, the call came. Bob had been moved to recovery. A doctor who had worked on him would speak with me.

I took a seat by the window in the room where I had started this long, now interminable-seeming day. I watched other doctors arrive to talk with other wives, husbands, and families and awaited whomever had been with Bob. I called Joey and Marilyn. I was guardedly relieved, climbing slowly out of the tangle of fears. I knew Bob was alive.

Dr. Ivanov, a tall, forty-something man, with a dark stubble, arrived with an even younger anesthesiologist, whose smiling face was framed by red curls. They seemed exhausted. Dr. Ivanov said Bob was "Fine," then excused himself. The anesthesiologist stayed long enough to explain they had been unable to close Bob because of heavy, uncontrollable internal bleeding. He said I could wait upstairs, where Bob was now. Once he was in the ICU, I could see him.

Here is what we learned later from Dr. Volpe's Operative Note.

Because of scarring, he could not tell whether one or two of my vessels were closed. He proceeded with the by-pass, though he was "not sure whether this will do any good." I was connected to a pump, which kept my blood circulating. My heart was "lifted out," the scarred areas excised, and segments of veins, which had been taken from each of my ankles, were grafted in to establish a new channel of flow.

My "formerly beautiful" mitral valve, while "grossly dilated" and scarred, was "not completely dead." It retained "excellent quality" tissue. He need not replace the valve; ringing it would do. This repair was so successful there was "absolutely no regurgitation." But I was "extremely bloody" and clotted so poorly, he suspected I had not stopped my Effient as instructed.

I was, he summed up, "very, very difficult to make clot... so much so that... we spent several hours in the operating room watching him and trying to get him to clot and this will be the big problem with this man post-op. Of course I have no experience with Effient and the experience I have had with Plavix has not been good, so it remains to be seen what will happen with this nice man, but the operation he received, the technical aspects of it, were perfectly satisfactory."

(Reading this for the first time, more than four years after it was written, still made me shiver. This "nice man" lying there. This technically "perfectly satisfactory" operation. This perfection and niceness resulting in this remaining unknown.)

83

I introduced myself at the nurse's station in the ICU. Bob's nurse was summoned and took me to him. He was sleeping, she explained, and wouldn't awake until morning. It was close to 8:00 p.m.

Seeing Bob was wonderful. He had good color and was breathing easily. The requisite tubes ran in and out of him, but in comparison to how he had looked after the second heart attack, it all seemed good. I asked if I could sleep in a chair beside him, but the nurse thought he'd be better served if I went to the hotel, had a decent night's rest, and had fresh energy for tomorrow, when he'd be awake. She was doing a double-shift and assured me she would take excellent care of him. She gave me the number to call, should I want an update at any point.

I sat with Bob a little longer, said our good night prayers solo, holding his hand, and kissed him. I was the only passenger on the last shuttle to the hotel. I called Marilyn, but, having already taken my sleeping pill, was too sleepy to talk. I fell asleep almost immediately. When I woke at 2:00 a.m., I called the hospital. Bob had woken briefly around midnight. The nurse had removed his breathing tube, and he was sleeping comfortably. He probably would not remember having awakened, but he was doing well.

I woke early, showered – and found a voicemail from Bob. I called back. It was thrilling to hear his voice. Again, I marveled at how much better he was doing than after his second M.I. I was on the first shuttle to the hospital. I felt so much better, I stopped at the cafeteria to pick up a few hard-boiled eggs, a fresh fruit salad, Greek yogurt, and a cup of Peet's French roast to take with me. I hadn't eaten one entire meal the day before.

XII. SQUIRRELS DO BETTER

Effient had been the problem. Being Plavix-resistant, I was fortunate it existed – but I was unfortunate its existence had been too brief for doctors to understand its workings. Patients came off Plavix a week before surgery. I had come off Effient – Dr. Volpe's suspicions to the contrary – ten days before mine. But even this had proved insufficient. I had bled so badly that they had coded me.

Adele and I learned this from the nurse who had assisted Dr. Ivanov, following Dr. Volpe's departure. We saw her my second day in the ICU, following my transfer from a dismal room, where I shared a TV with another patient, to a room in which I had my own. She was a trim, no-nonsense brunette, who looked like she knocked down triathlons like pints of beer.

"You mean, like Code Blue?" I said. Maybe she had meant Code Grey. But that summons security when a patient attacks a doctor, and I had been in no condition for that. Maybe she had meant Code Pink. But that is when someone swipes an infant from Pediatrics, for which I had no inclination.

"Dr. Ivanov saved your life," she said.

We had been disappointed to learn that he would be attending me for the rest of my stay. Dr. Ivanov, frankly, had a bedside manner which made Dr. Caligari's seem rosy. He had already informed us, "It will be six months before we know if the surgery did any good. Only one-third of patients improve. One-third remain the same, and one-third worsen." We had welcomed that information as would a birthday balloon a porcupine.

But now we were all thanks and gratitude.

I had a twelve-inch scar down the middle of my chest and, below that, what looked like a second belly button, where a tube had pierced me. I had a five-inch scar on the inner aspect of each lower leg, where the veins had been harvested for the bypass. My right shoulder ached from a muscle pulled when I had been spread apart for better viewing. The breathing tube had re-scratched my throat and re-started my coughing. (All this would hurt less than the bed sore I developed on my butt from being forced to lie in one position.)

My biggest problem was being forbidden to put pressure on the wires that knit my chest together. I could not use my arms to boost or steady myself while getting in or out of bed. I could not use them when I sat on or rose from a chair. I could not reach behind myself to pull a t-shirt on or off or to wash or dry my back. I could not lift anything heavier than a newspaper.

On the third day, we moved upstairs from the ICU to Recovery. Bob's room held one bed and one chair. Its view was of a slice of park. Its TV's possibilities were unexpanded by cable. The first morning there, I overheard a doctor discuss Bob's heart with residents he was leading on rounds. Everything he said about the consequences of Bob's damaged heart being unable to deliver an adequate blood supply worried me. I had forgotten that the doctor's job was to teach his residents everything he could. If we had the recovery we hoped for, what he said made no difference.

But I was doing fine at the Kabuki. I found it easier to sleep there than when I had been running back and forth between home and Sutter. I became used to the shuttle. I discovered an organic grocery where I could get food for the day, which the nurses let me stash in their refrigerator. The neighborhood was rich with restaurants and cafes and bookstores. Sometimes I talked to my sister as I walked. Other times I went to a nearby park, atop a hill, from which I could see the city spread out before me. It was a familiar and also foreign country. I had almost hour-by-hour recall of Bob's time in Sutter, but now the days blurred together. It wasn't better or worse, just different.

Sutter had become almost a second home, but California Pacific remained a place apart. It brought back the 1960s though, and my early days in San Francisco. Every block evoked people I had known and experiences I'd had. On my walks, I contemplated the familiar street names and buildings and compared them to the now-different context. Although "then" had excited, with endless possibilities and dreams and a feeling of invulnerability, as a person, with Bob, I was much more solid "now." In the '60s I had been searching for everything, a profession, writing success, the life I would live, and the person I would live it with. Now I had that person and that life and had lived it, fully, for forty-plus years.

Fillmore Street resonated most deeply. Most of my various haunts, like the Royal Café, no longer existed. There, in 1965, for $.99-to-$1.99, you could feast on soup, salad, fries or mashed, broccoli or green beans, liver, steak or veal, ice cream, and beverage. The sign, "Superior Food," in the window had been an exaggerated misnomer, but it was good and affordable and suited me and my then-boyfriend, a troubled and brilliant revolutionary. He was trying to free me from my capitalist family and repressed sexuality, while I was trying to coax him back to college, which he'd quit, freshman year, after his mother had killed his siblings and left his father and him for dead before killing herself.

From the park, I could see across San Francisco to the Panhandle, where I'd danced to the Grateful Dead. I ran through the city in my head, connecting all the roads I'd driven and walked and made memories before Bob arrived. It had only been a few-year digression before I was back on track with him, but feeling the distance between those years and now gave me an unexpected boost. I had needed those experiences, but what I had found was even better than I had hoped.

Once, in the mid-'70s, when I was a therapist, I'd sat on a bench with a view like the one I had now, beside a woman I was treating. She had been bent on killing herself then but had gone on to live a couple good decades, in a good relationship, with good work, before dying of natural causes. As I stood up to return to Cal Pacific, I thought of all the progress she had made in those decades and that Bob had made in the last week and felt a bounce in my step, knowing we would soon be going home.

As Bob gained strength, we took longer and longer slow walks, out of the pocket of like-rooms and their nurses' station, to the straightaway hall that connected to other clusters of rooms. One day we found where Bob had slept *the night before surgery. I was glad we had gotten past that. Another day we heard, then saw a hospital-gowned patient practically sprint past us. We joked about what he might be chasing but later found out he was the recipient of a second heart transplant. The first had gone bad, but his dash was a positive visual of the possible.*

Again, nurses, techs and therapists bled, X-rayed and scanned me. Again, my blood pressure, temperature and pulse were measured, day and night. I came off the drip I had been receiving to stimulate my blood flow. I came off my pacer wires. But the ICU's restrictions held. To do more, I would have to hoist the Mack truck Dr. Volpe had warned of from my chest.

But cardio-rehab had strengthened my legs, making my "no hands" maneuvers easier. I rose and sat and rose and sat. I walked halls and climbed stairs. I did the assigned exercises and requested more. If my blood pressure registered too low for me to be allowed out of bed, I exercised while lying down and had it re-taken.

Dr. Volpe visited for the first – and only – time, five days after the operation. When he entered, I was exercising my lungs by drawing air through a tube, every inhalation an attempt to force a marker to the top of a plastic cylinder. "Squirrels do better," he said, smiling at my best effort. He snatched the device and rang its gong. I was prepared to hear that, in his spare time, he sang tenor for the San Francisco Opera. Instead, he announced my recovery had progressed so well I would be discharged a day earlier than expected.

But Adele's and my elation did not survive the afternoon. An echo-cardiogram, whose results Dr. Volpe had not seen, showed that my heart's left ventricular's function, with an ejection fraction of 30, was too weak to expel the fluid sluiced into me during surgery. Dr. Ivanov ordered me returned to the ICU for monitoring while IVs fed me medication to strengthen my heart and help me void. It was frightening to be back in ICU. It was frightening not to know how long I would be there.

It felt terrible to see Bob's spirits crushed.

I felt duped again by Dr. Volpe's unwarranted high spirits and overly optimistic assessment. I had been in the room when the echo was done, and its audio now seemed as foreboding as the turbulence of approaching rapid waters. My strongest upset stemmed from the words "not strong enough to void." I knew that was imperative for recovery. Again, a doctor with medical students in-tow paid an annoying visit. Again, I caught a discouraging sentence. Bob's heart might be too damaged to ever properly oxygenate his heart and limbs. We had to hope the drugs would turn the tide. We hoped to have a fighting chance for Bob's body to do the rest.

Meanwhile, a minor problem reared. I had only booked one week at the Kabuki, and when I said I would need a room for a second, they didn't have one. A psychologist/basketball buddy of Bob's offered me a couch in his house across town, but just before I was to decamp, the hotel came up with a suite in its basement. It had no interior walls, just curtained-off compartments. A gigantic mirror hung over the bed. Neither the shower nor the TV worked. Its strangeness seemed to reflect the world into which Bob and I had been forced. But its nearness to him overrode its discontents, and the following day the Kabuki came up with something more normal.

The ICU medication worked so well I twice wet my bed.

The next day I returned to Recovery. I was weak. I coughed. I went on and off different medications. No one mentioned discharge, but the whispers of doom vanished too.

I continued to walk and exercise. If confidence and macho daring pushed me to over test my arms, I re-trenched once Adele caught me. My appetite was good. I tried nearly everything the daily menus offered, but only the Italian dinner warranted a second chance. I watched snippets of ballgames. Adele snuck me a double espresso, which lifted my spirits further – but set my left leg jiggling uncontrollably. She proudly presented me a used copy of Kate Atkinson's newly published *Left Early Took the Dog*. (Later she confessed that, since I would have objected if I had known she had bought it new, she had the clerk mark it as if it was used and scuff it, so I would not suspect her duplicity.)

Bob's second weekend in Cal Pacific, Dr. Fleur visited. Returning from vacation, she'd found Dr. Volpe's message that he'd discharged him. Only after not be able to reach us at home had she inquired further. She'd tried to come earlier, but emergencies had intervened. It was good for us to think she was coming and then, when she couldn't, to look forward to her again. When she got there, her blonde hair loose, lovely in skin-fit jeans and gorgeous sweater, we were not disappointed. She bubbled over with positive feelings.

As a bonus for me, she loved my haircut.

Dr. Fleur said nothing suggested the surgery had failed. It was natural that its shock would traumatize my heart; recovery was equally likely. Even if I became no better than I had been, options remained. She found one clear positive. "Everyone agrees you've proved yourself a good candidate for a transplant."

Which, while welcome news, was not exactly "I'll see you again in five years."

I came up with a second. For six months I'd teetered along the high wire of not knowing if I would need surgery. Now I had the stability of putting that behind me.

Two days later, – my ejection fraction up to 34 – nine medications in tow – I was home.

XIII. THE MESSAGE IN THE BOWL

Our bed embraced me like an old and long unseen friend. Our TV held all the entertainment I could stand. I was fed from our refrigerator – nonfat yogurt and nonfat muffin – no one else's. But it would take Adele's urging to get me on my feet.

Once Bob was set up on the bed, with a snack and the TV remote, I went into action.

I unpacked, did a laundry, made a grocery list, found a folding table to hold our medical supplies, and put the medications in order, separating his night meds from his morning. Marilyn helped me assemble a shower bench, which she'd picked up for us at a medical supply store. It anchored on the side of the tub and extended outward, making it safe for Bob, by sitting down and slinging his legs over the edge, to slip under the shower without putting weight on his arms. She assisted with adjusting a commode to the proper height and positioning it bedside so Bob wouldn't have to walk far to urinate, reducing his chance of falling. The phone rang often, friends and family welcoming us home.

Hospital time had seemed vast, slow, each day an eternity; now it accelerated, the next thing to do waiting impatiently for me to finish what preceded it. I tried my mantra from an old Breema class, "No hurry; no pause." It did not help.

At three that first afternoon, I joined Bob on the bed. He watched an A's game with the sound off, while I was on hold with the hospital about a discrepancy in his discharge medication I wanted to check out. It was a blissful time. Our mobile rose and dipped, the changing light illuminating our art anew. Home felt like heaven.

Later, when I suggested a walk around the house, Bob wanted to go outside. Navigating the stairs, getting into the car, driving to flat ground was more than daunting. Even with several rest stops, the walk only lasted ten minutes and left us both exhausted, Bob from physical exertion, and both of us from tension. Dr. Volpe's warnings that the early stages of recovery would be challenging had been right.

When we got home, we decided to postpone showering. I gave Bob a sponge bath, cleaned his incision sites with no-rinse soap, a helpful donation from our discharge nurse. I treated the bedsore as I'd been taught, took his blood pressure, made us a light supper. We both ate on the bed. Sleep beckoned, but we made it through half the first episode of the new season of Boardwalk Empire.

I slept in disposable shorts because I lacked bladder control. I wore support stockings to prevent clots in my legs. I could not bathe, or dress myself, or drive, or lift over ten pounds. I could read newspapers or magazines but could not concentrate enough for books. I could not hold onto thoughts long enough to write. (It took me ten days to make my first post-discharge journal entry.) My weight had dropped to 160 (and would drop to 147 over the next eight weeks, which I had not weighed since ninth grade.) I was so thin my wedding ring slipped off my finger. (I would have felt so badly if I lost it that I bought a snugger-fitting silver one to wear between it and the nearest knuckle as a guard.)

Since gripping railings – and risking throwing my weight upon my chest, if I slipped – was forbidden, descending our front steps was risky. I went out only for doctors' appointments or walks, and, when walking, I rested every few minutes. The idea that I must walk thirty minutes, every day, for the rest of my life was difficult to comprehend.

Bob's first shower left him clean, but I was soaked. So was the floor and half-a-dozen towels. "We'll get better at this," I said. "I'll wear my shower cap and rain coat." That got a smile. But two days later, when we tried again and I stopped Bob from doing something he felt capable of, he snapped at me, his anger upsetting us both.

The next day, Victoria, the home care team leader, an LVN, examined Bob. The orientation appointment ran over an hour, as she took a detailed history and copied into her tablet the long list of Bob's medications. She found no problems, but issued lengthy warnings of things to watch out for. When she heard of our difficulties with the shower, she told us we were entitled to a helper, which was welcome news.

On my first post-surgical visit with Dr. Fleur, the waiting room was decorated for Halloween. Orange or black paper bats and witches hung upon the walls. They did not register as entirely inappropriate since, Dr. Fleur explained, one of my medicines, Digoxin, stemmed from a discovery by a witch 600 years before. It seemed people with edema – swelling – came to her for treatment and she found that a tea made from foxgloves increased peeing, which alleviated their problem. True, some of her patients died; but some got better, so, with further experimentation, digitalis was born.

Dr. Fleur said my bed sore was healing beautifully. She encouraged me to raise my weight to 165. She cut my Metoprolol and Ramipril dosages in half, and because I was so thin and, seemingly, had "no cholesterol," took me off Lipitor. Since I was "not growing breasts," I could continue Spironolactone; otherwise she would have cancelled that too.

But the overall picture had not clarified. We would not know for months if the surgery had benefitted me or if I would need something more.

We were disappointed to hear Bob's heart might need more work, even though Dr. Fleur's excitement about transplants had been stirred by a conference she'd attended where the latest developments in pumps had been demonstrated on an eighty-eight-year-old. I bolstered my spirits by recalling the happy fellow who had jogged by Bob and I in the hospital hall with his new heart. We then laughed about how he'd looked half our age – and probably was.

"Heal and get healthy," Dr. Fleur said, but the seeming extremity of the word "transplant" hung another cloud over us. We left, resolving to clear it away, and return to our hope that it wouldn't be necessary. We had already established tiny islands of progress – fewer and shorter rest periods on walks; wound care and sponge baths in the bathroom, instead of on the bed; meals at the table – which had made us feel Bob would make the top third Dr. Ivanov had mentioned.

We encouraged each other with positive feelings, both of us having the same goal, "Best recovery possible."

Friends said I looked and sounded better than they expected. But LVNs, RVNs, occupational therapists, and physical therapists visited so often, I felt like Humpty Dumpty attended by all the king's men.

Victoria constantly encouraged me. She termed my heart "steady." My lungs lacked "funny noises," and the surgical scars on my legs looked "more like paper cuts than incisions." "Celebrate each small victory," she said, "because you've worked hard for them. Some people assume an operation is a silver bullet. They won't exercise or change their diet. You're the healthiest patient on my route. You're the only one who answers the doorbell to let me in."

I did not feel like celebrating. I increased my walks, until I could do twenty-five minutes; but my systolic blood pressure still registered in the low eighties. I was tired, mornings, evenings, and after each walk. My chest, shoulder, and rear end still hurt.

I wanted to do everything I could myself, because "doing" gave me a feeling of strength and control, but I also learned when to put that aside. Since I wasn't yet comfortable leaving Bob alone long enough to do a significant grocery shop and/or get a much needed physical workout, I accepted offerings that allowed for that. Even a short, brisk walk could revive me. Marilyn gave me those chances most weekends and on her non-teaching weekdays. Sometimes, by the weekend, I already had the groceries in the house, and I was free to go the Claremont for a full workout, shower and shampoo. Bob and she enjoyed their times together, watching sports and discussing movies, while I restocked the cabinets and refrigerator and replenished my endorphins. One night, when Bob stood shivering as he prepared to shower, I had the idea of warming the towels in the dryer before he undressed. That helped both for showers and wound care, and I congratulated myself for my brilliance.

Our shower aide, recruited by Victoria, fit us perfectly. Carmella was a tall, strong Brazilian, who easily aligned with Bob's strengths and needs and exuded confidence in a fashion that quieted my anxieties. She taught us well, and his showers became a pleasure. She sang songs and told us funny, sad stories about her life. Brazilian boys had been intimidated by her height, and she was rarely asked out. She accused me of having stolen a tall one, and we all laughed.

I felt immense gratitude to all our allies, the friends who visited, the people who cared in e-mails and phone calls, the folks at the club who inquired, the checkers at Andronico's who wondered where my husband was.

But the sheer number of home care visits drove me crazy. Each visitor took the same information, pecking it into her ancient Palm Pilot. They updated each visit, but often had lost the preceding one, which meant having to start from the beginning: medications, hospitalizations, and history. Geri, our regular nurse, never looked me in the eye. On one occasion, she caused us undue worry, by insisting Bob's bed sore had worsened, and starting a time-consuming comedy of errors to switch him onto a heavy duty antibiotic, leaving, she said, messages for it at both Dr. Fleur's and Dr. Zipp's, then going off duty for days, while I unsuccessfully pestered both our pharmacies for word of its authorization. When I was finally able to reach the doctors' offices, one had no record of Geri's call and the other had been unable to reach her for the clarification it needed. Finally Victoria bailed us out with a special visit and examination to assure us all was well. The next time Geri appeared, she didn't draw enough blood to cover the tests Dr. Fleur had ordered and had to return to stick Bob again.

Bob's bruising and bleeding, each time he bumped himself, bothered me. And I injured myself too. My back spasmed when making the bed or carrying bags of groceries upstairs from the car. My hands cramped chopping vegetables. My legs, feet and arms cramped as I slept. I was continually recovering from something. And through all this, I had to fit in a dermatology appointment, eye check-up, and visits to the dentist and chiropractor.

One day, I fell hard against a wooden chest when hurrying to make the bed before Bob returned from the bathroom. I didn't tell him. Nothing upsets him more than my hurting myself doing something he would have if he was well.

That afternoon, I reluctantly agreed to Bob's taking a walk with a buddy. I was trying to curb my tendency to be over-controlling, and my back was bothering me. I prepped dinner while they were gone and tried to straighten out another medication snafu. Dr. Fleur's office hadn't faxed a prescription to one pharmacy and had faxed the wrong one to another. Bob arrived home exhausted, having over-done it.

After supper, I was silently giving thanks we'd made it through the day, when I found him, half-on, half-off the commode, listing to one side, eyes closed. I called his name. His head slumped further forward. I ran to him, terrified he'd had a stroke.

I called "Bob," again and reached for the cell phone. His arm and leg twitched, and his eyes opened.

"What are you doing?"

"Calling 911. Something happened to you."

"Don't call," he said, in a clear voice, sitting up straight. "I got dizzy and had a sharp pain in my knee, like I get sometimes going up stairs. Sorry I worried you."

When I asked him to, he stuck out his tongue and held up both arms.

I prayed not-calling was the right decision.

Where Adele had learned how to test for strokes, I never knew. But it was a handy talent.

The next day, I felt cocky enough to suggest we take our walk at the Claremont.

We did twenty minutes, circling a route above the parking lot. Then, fortified by the protein bar and water bottle Adele had equipped me with, I lay on a chaise and read the *Times*, while she exercised more.

When I'd had all the sun my dermatologist allotted, I hauled my scarred chest and flabby arms into the locker room for their first public viewing. I topped off my efforts with an unattended shower, cautiously choosing the smallest stall, so if I slipped I would collide against – and hopefully brace myself with – a wall.

Adele and I celebrated the outing with a vegi-Chinese lunch, followed by a trip to the French, where I had half a single espresso, my first caffeine since leaving the hospital.

Sometimes recovery felt like a baseball season, a bad day followed by a good one, no one winning them all. Bob wanting to go to the club seemed like we were beginning a hot streak. Just the week before, he'd felt too vulnerable to be seen and asked questions. Now we joked about who'd be first to ask about his weight loss. The ride over, across campus, past the frat and sorority houses, through the mansion district, listening to jazz was pure delight. I remembered a dream in which I'd stared at an empty bottle of Joy in our spice rack. Now I felt well-seasoned with it.

I watched Bob lying on his chaise, as I worked the treadmill. Knowing he was with me was better than music for raising my energy level and heart rate. A woman, who has a locker next to mine and regularly inquired about him, shot me a thumbs-up from her recumbent bike. The locker room had always seemed a minefield of unwelcome possibilities-to-talk. In the past I'd been wary of the disease-operation-recovery conversations that filled the place. But Bob's illness had shifted my relationship to that aspect of the community. Now that we had our share of misfortune, I appreciated the concern, and I had gained many new best-friends-of-the-day-or-week. Sometimes all it took was a look for me to launch into an uncomfortable-making more-than-I-wanted-to-say. But other times it felt good to connect and unburden.

The Most Annoying Question award went to an overweight physician who asked why Bob was so skinny and accused me of not feeding him. I wanted to punch her.

The next visit to Dr. Fleur produced no bells and whistles. I was eating right, though still losing weight, exercising appropriately, and things were coming along. She took me off one diuretic, reduced the dose of another and started me on something new. She still didn't want me working out with weights, but she okayed my returning to cardio-rehab. When I said I did not feel ready, she wrote the order anyway, so I could begin when I wanted.

I was not to see her for five weeks. It would be our longest separation. Adele and I felt so close to her we were disappointed she did not invite us to Thanksgiving.

We'd waited an hour for Dr. Fleur in a small examination room. Bob fell asleep on the table, but I didn't even have a book to read to pass the time. She poked her head in twice to apologize, and, after a half-hour, I left the door ajar to create at least the illusion of fresh air.

When it was finally our turn, Dr. Fleur seemed delighted to see us and gave me a big hug. She listened to Bob's heart and lungs and remarked on his improvement. His latest blood work was excellent, and we left feeling uplifted by her warmth and high spirits.

And her not mentioning transplants.

The next day, after promising Adele I would call as soon as I arrived, I set out for the French alone. My route wound gradually downhill. It was shaded by redwoods and pines, the sun sliced the fog into illuminated ribbons. The grab-bag architecture of the houses – brown shingle, stucco and Victorian – delighted. Their yards' adornments – ceramic frog, wood burl bear, tuna cans carved into fish – entranced. Each garden fought to out-marvel its neighbor in color and design, through shrub and flower, succulent and creeper. I read "Life is good" at the bottom of a ceramic bowl, left out with water for passing pets.

I said "Hello" to everyone I saw. I sang snatches of songs from *Oklahoma* and Bob Dylan. I murmured Corky's "blessed-healing-loved" mantra. The penumbra of all I had been through enriched each moment. Taking a curbside table, I smiled at the assembled by whom I was surrounded.

"Are you feeling better than before surgery?" Jennifer, a massage therapist, asked me.

"Well, I don't have surgery to worry about, for one thing," I said. It might be the Lexapro; but if attitude was key, I was fine.

Hell, if attitude was key, I would soon be flying.

XIV. THE BLESSED

*I watched Bob fill journal pages at home and yellow, lined legal pads when
we were at the French or Berkeley Espresso. His efforts produced sentences,
then paragraphs, and finally pages, all hopeful signs for him. For weeks I only
read, but one day I imagined rendering each chapter of* Mold Central, *that
humorous horror story, in a way that perseverance and humanity triumphed,
like what seemed to be happening with Bob and me. Maybe, I thought, I'd
feel better if I could find forgiveness for our beleaguered contractor, his felonious
workers, the incompetent architect, Berkeley's insane building codes, and the
decent subcontractors whom we paid, since our contractor couldn't, in order for
the work to continue. The result, I comfortingly realized, our rebuilt back stairs,
allowed a beautiful view of the bay and a warm, sunny exercise toy for Bob to
walk up and down.*

*I fantasized turning this story into a tale of fortitude and spiritual victory,
while retaining its bite and laughter. For a few days, I felt alive, excited, and
as hopeful as Bob. I carried my journal to the café, in case inspiration ripened
into output, but inspiration only added turbulence to the relentless flow of my
daily concerns. I ground to a halt, drowned in the sheer number of things I had
to do after we left the café, and before I'd returned to it, I'd find a week or more
had passed. Bob encouraged me to talk about my disappointment, but I kept to
myself how lost I felt, existing only in the role of caretaker, wanting to do what I
was doing, but wondering when and how I would recover other parts of my self.*

At the Claremont, I worked toward the consecutive ten-minute stints on
the three machines I would need to do at rehab.

But between my medication schedule and my exercise sessions, I
could not establish a relaxed, give-and-take rhythm. On occasion, I
rebelled against Adele's control over matters, big or small. I wanted days
off. I wanted to put my shoes on myself. I wanted to carry groceries
to the car. But once I satisfied my pride by asserting independence, I
accepted her limits.

Slowly, my feelings improved. I completed pieces for *Broad Street* about the Saturday matinees of my childhood and my history as a boxing fan. I built my caffeine tolerance up, from half an espresso to my former customary short double. Adele and I went out to lunch. (At a vegetarian Chinese restaurant where we'd eaten for decades, the couple who ran it tailored dishes especially for me, a gesture which touched us both.) I hoped that as I re-established familiarity with these acts, I would accept them as commonplace, rather than as tests or adventures. I hoped to enjoy the here and now, rather than worry about unknowns in the future.

"Dr. Ivanov said you could have twenty years," Adele said, "if things went well."

"I think I am going to make it," I said.

"I've been feeling the same but have been afraid to say it. I'm not scared every moment I will lose you."

We agreed we felt "Blessed." It was the first time we had shared that word.

The evening before our post-hospital visit with Dr. Volpe to hear his assessment, I needed two tranquilizers and a sleeping pill. I was out so solidly I wet the bed.

At four, Bob woke me with the announcement the sheets were soaked. I stripped the bed and got him cleaned up and into a fresh t-shirt and underpants. I made my side of the bed for him and left his side to dry and air out. The mattress had been spared, except for a bit of dampness I took care of with my hair dryer.

When Bob woke, a few hours later, I made his breakfast and washed the heavy mattress cover. It filled the washer and had to be repositioned each time the load became unbalanced. It took several cycles to dry. While we waited for Robert to arrive to drive us to San Francisco, I opened the windows to air out the room. I'd been so busy, I hadn't given a thought to whether the appointment would leave us feeling encouraged or discouraged – of even if we'd make it there and back. I rubbed my eyes, found an eyelash on my finger, and wished for good news.

Hadley, Dr. Volpe's medical assistant, saw us. She said my surgical wounds, chest and legs, were fine and pronounced my heart and lungs excellent.

She explained that, during the surgery, I had received ten-pounds of fluids, some of which my cells retained and had to come out. But I had also lost fifteen-to-twenty pounds of muscle, which had to be regained. In two weeks, I could begin exercising with two-pound dumb bells, one arm at a time. I could drive now – but not on rainy roads or crowded streets, where I would be more likely to have an accident and strike my chest on the steering wheel. I could quit the support stockings. She gave me her direct phone number and e-mail address if we had questions. With that, I was discharged, no need to return.

I dozed off before we reached the bridge. I napped when we got home. Then, at night, I needed the sleeping pill, the tranquilizers, and an hour-and-a-half of meditation to sleep.

We treated Robert to lunch and a frozen yogurt in San Francisco to celebrate Hadley's words. We stopped by the book store that had roughed up the Atkinson novel I had passed off as "Used" to say "Thank you."

It was special being back on Fillmore with Bob. We held hands, breathed the fresh air, and felt grateful. How I'd longed for this wonderfulness when I'd been alone and frightened, or clutched my cell phone as I'd updated my brother or sister on the latest crisis or progress or both.

At home, everything felt bright and shiny clean. I set about reassembling the bed in a relaxed and mindful way. As I did, I gave myself credit for dealing with frustrations. I was learning to take a job well done to heart and let it inspire me for whatever came next. I asked Bob if he'd resume use of his padded underpants at night until he got his medicines and sleep cycle sorted out.

He said, "Yes."

In mid-November I returned to cardio-rehab for a re-re-re-orientation. Medicare covered only thirty-six visits, but each time you had another "incident" you could begin again. It was not a bonus for which to strive, but it was nice to have it available.

Pam, the interview nurse, said I looked great. But she had last seen me when she had been working on the ICU when I'd lain in my coma. And I'd not yet heard any patient told by anyone at rehab, "Boy, you look like shit!"

"You may not feel normal for a year," she said. "The heart adjusts to a faulty valve, so it must relearn how to behave with a repaired one. Since your malfunction came from a sudden event, rather than a long, gradual decline, yours may rehabilitate sooner."

My preferred late morning class was full, as was my second choice, so I'd settled on an 8:30 AM, with the option to transfer if space opened elsewhere. I remembered how rehab's routine could bore me and how my competitive juices could be unhealthily stirred by others' performance on their machines.

I promised myself to do better.

I felt frightened. My earlier experiences when Bob was in rehab had been replaying unpleasantly in my dreams and waking hours. I knew I'd be vulnerable to panic if I took a walk while he worked out, each step away from him increasing my own heart rate, a siren in the distance setting it pounding like war drums. But if I stayed inside, I'd feel there was not enough air to breath, and if I read the books on the shelves, I'd worry about the diseases they described.

The 8:30 class seemed like folly. Bob would have to get up early to be ready, and his blood pressure would not likely risen to the level necessary for his morning meds, so I'd worry about him exerting himself without them on board. And, perhaps selfishly, I resented losing my morning time, when I had my most energy to prep meals and make the day go better.

After the orientation appointment, on impulse, we walked up Telegraph Avenue to Moe's to browse for used books. Bob scored a review copy of Joan Didion's Blue Nights, about the death of her daughter, which had followed soon upon the death of Didion's husband, for us to read aloud. (Death-upon-death might seem an odd choice, but we so admired Didion's artistry, we assumed it would carry this load.) The spontaneity and normalcy of our action felt remarkable and went a long way toward settling me down from the agitation I'd experienced inside the cardio building.

Halfway back to the car, Bob admitted he'd reached his limit. I was pleased by his ability to say "Enough." He waited on a bus stop bench while I got the car.

I made angel hair pasta, with scallops, garlic, and Italian parsley for dinner, doubling the olive oil to add calories. (It was delicious, but left Bob too full for dessert, so I wasn't sure he came out ahead for the day.) We watched a Jean Harlow comedy; but when its manic intensity became too much, switched to an Oakland Raiders game, until Bob pronounced that "a lost cause." I noted how anti-depressants had helped Bob bypass the apprehensions he'd had, even before he'd become a heart patient. Now and then, it felt like the Bob I'd known was gone. Sometimes when he smiled at me, simply from a pleasant thought, I had to ask what he was thinking. He had paradoxically become a happier man amidst our horrors. I wondered if I should be on anti-depressants too.

Before sleep, we discussed feeling a shared vulnerability, not yet knowing how much the operation had helped and realizing the cardio-rehab work-outs, with the monitoring of his heart and the testing further down the road, would be part of finding out. We recognized we were changing in response to the crisis, always grateful for the positives, making increased energy available to reach the best result. Everything seemed better.

XV. CAKE

On November 15, my mother died.

She had taken a sip of water, lain down her head – and was gone. A graveside ceremony would be held, my brother said, in a South Jersey cemetery, near Alliance, where our father's father's father had settled after fleeing Russia in 1890 – and where our father and sister already lay. One set of our cousins might attend. None of the others felt sufficiently connected. None of my mothers' surviving contemporaries felt fit enough to go. Nor did I. I regretted that. I regretted that I had not written this week. I regretted I had not called. Not that any of that would have made a difference. There was always something to regret.

My mother, I thought, would not have minded my absence. Her own mother had died when she was a child, and she had little faith in ritual. When the doctors had not thought my father would survive his heart attack, in 1969, and I'd flown in from California, she had told me to return, once I had said "Good bye." After all, she'd reasoned, what could I do? He took my departure as a good sign, thinking there was no way I would have left if he was dying – and rallied.

Now my mother was gone too. She had been supportive, generous, strong. But she had been gone for years. This had led to frustration and anger but not to hope. There had been no hope. Still my brother and I could feel good that we had left her in her apartment, where she had felt safe and well cared for, and there was nothing to alarm her. Adele said she had found her caring and smart and easy to talk to. "I even liked what I didn't like about her," she said.

My mother had been my last contact with a generation which had once been the most influential upon me. Now it had joined the departed, existing only as memories – acts shared, anecdotes recalled – sensations, visions, feelings – through which we define who we are or remember how we came to be. I was nearly seventy and on my own.

That night I took two tranquilizers, managed four hours' sleep – and wet the bed again.

"That," Adele said, "was from a boy who could not shed his tears."

I'd written to Bob's mother every week. We knew she didn't read our letters anymore and were unsure what she took in when they were read to her by others. Her nurses said she seemed most attached to the envelopes, which she'd hold and run her fingers across. Could she feel our love? I hoped so. Did the envelopes remind her of the paper dolls she cut out to play with as a child because her family could not afford real ones? When we called and she spoke a few precious words, it felt like we were there in her mind.

Bob and I each wrote something to be read at her graveside. This was mine:

Friends ask if I will miss writing to you. I know I will. But on this sad day, I delay beginning and write this.

Our correspondence over the years had so many phases – recipes, dreams, a shared enjoyment of your son, our lives, my excitements over Roger Federer, personal and family news – I know it brought us both pleasure. Even when you chose to stop responding, claiming your tremors made your handwriting unreadable, I could still "know" what you would have said. Smart pithy words, Yiddishisms, expressions of generosity, and conveyances of the feeling you were on our side. These letters were perhaps the way we got to know and love each other most deeply.

Occasionally, you rattled my cage. One day when you were visiting us, I asked, "Did you love me at first sight?" You answered that you'd been surprised by Bob's choice. You had expected someone more like yourself – but you had grown to love me. The boldness of your assertion startled me. I tried to hold it against you in my black-humored way, but it became a treasured moment, always bringing a deep smile to Bob and me when I'd retell the story.

You gave me many wonderful gifts I never tire of thanking you for, from Bob, to the needle-point pillows your hands, time and love stitched, to the afghans that warm us at night, to the sweaters that are still complimented. Thanks, once more. The washer-and-dryer you bought us, which I dubbed "Strong Mothers," still do the job. We fought for a decade before I accepted your offer, classic daughter-mother fare. Thanks for persevering and letting me reach the end of a battle. You gave me the chance to grow up and be the loving, loyal daughter and adult friend, I hadn't quite accomplished to be with my own parents.

All my friends envied me for having the best mother-in-law in the world.
I'll miss you, Mom, and remember you well and always.
I'll end my usual way: Lots of love and a HUGE hug!

On the day of the service, while Rebecca was being buried, Bob and I lit a candle
and had a meditative "sit" on our bed.

My mother's death had disturbed my already shaky sleep patterns; and low blood pressure readings had thrown off my morning medication schedule, so rushing out of the house to get to 8:30 rehab sessions seemed unwise. I needed time to adjust and asked what was available if I began after Thanksgiving. They had an early afternoon slot, and I grabbed it.

By the time I began rehab, I was more than ready. I had a settled, soothing routine. Every morning I went to the French. I read the paper. I wrote. Sometimes I chatted. Then after lunch and my rehab session, if Adele hadn't taken a walk, we'd go to the Claremont, and I'd sunbathe and shower, while she exercised on aerobic machines. On non-rehab days, Adele and I went there, and we'd both work-out. I had become proud to be the skinniest guy in the locker room. Which did not prevent my admiring my developing muscles.

Once a woman remarked how much she liked watching the two of us interact, and we realized the affection we demonstrated might seem unusual for a couple our age. But it was natural to us.

Bob had loosened up about whom he told about his heart troubles. He seemed to
feel strengthened by sharing these war stories. I did not do as well. I would find
myself in intimate discussions with someone who asked about him, and end up
shaken by the re-immersion in the experience.

I continued to think about Bob's mother too. On our first visit east, after his
father's death, she'd told me she'd been angry at me for "abandoning" him during
the last months of his life by not talking on the phone with him. I had written
letters but had left the calls to Bob.

106

I said I had thought it important for Bob and his Dad to talk as much as possible and apologized for all hurt feelings. She forgave me with the warning, "Do not ever do that again!" I assumed she'd meant to "her," and I could feel I had managed what I had promised.

When I mentioned this to Bob's cousin Elizabeth, an artist, therapist, and student of all Levin family foibles, she had linked to Rebecca's immediate lack of trust in me, to the loss of her mother, at age five, and loss of her daughter at the same age. Rebecca, Elizabeth said, had needed to trust and then love me; and my "abandonment" of Herb had allowed her distrust to rise once more. The good years in our relationship that followed seemed part of a "healing" of both of us.

Healing, I thought, was a long and strange and uncertain process.

Each week, as in my previous rehab stints, I increased my speed and effort level on the bikes and treadmill. My blood pressure sometimes read in the seventies – but other times broke 120. The highs were rewarded by a staff member's "Very nice." The lows were dismissed as the product of my meds or my having been at rest. I regained ten pounds of muscle. I steadily reduced my intake of sleeping pills, until I could get my eight hours without them. I stopped the absorbent undies. If my back ached after a work-out, I told myself, "Don't worry. It is not your heart." If I felt dizzy when I stood, I reassured myself by remembering that many similar dizzinesses had passed without harm. When it became time to pay my annual dues, I went "Inactive" with the State Bar with no deep feeling of loss.

In fact, my life felt fuller and richer than ever. Was it, I wondered, because my heart was pumping more oxygen to my brain? Was it because of my meds, or a spiritual breakthrough, or simply because of the removal of the pressures of the law? "I feel embarrassed to say it," I told Adele, "but if I do get twenty years, this may be the best thing that could have happened to me."

"Each day I wake up feeling good seems like a gift," she said. "I had no idea we would get through this, or what we would be like if we did. This is beyond my hopes."

But there were concerns.

I struck my head against a cabinet door and bled and bled. If I stretched my arms too far to the side or raised them directly above my head, Adele corrected me. If she saw me lift a ten-pound bag, she became frightened I would injure myself. If I went out on a cold day in a light jacket, she worried I would catch a chill. I knew she was trying to protect me, but I felt constrained. And she was furious that my too-casual attitude was forcing her to take responsibility for me – and fearful she would be blamed by others if anything went wrong.

One evening, she spotted me fingering a half-inch-long bump on my chest, near my incision, which had been sore for two days. After I had poo-poo-ed its significance, I agreed to the ER.

"It's not 'chest pain,'" I corrected the admittance clerk. "It's a pain *on* my chest."

He rushed me in anyway.

"No good can come of this," I said to Adele, as they wired me to an EKG.

But after reviewing it and an X-ray, the doctor diagnosed, "A migrating wire. Common after surgery. The pain will resolve, once scar tissue forms around it."

But what about when the season changes, I thought, and it wants to return from whence it came?

I could see Bob was recovering. I could say, "Look forward to seeing you in the morning," a part of our pre-sleep "prayer" and anticipate delight when we both awoke. But every time he bled, I'd recall my father literally passing out when I cut myself, and my mother's raging that I was trying to kill myself or her, by using my body in ordinary ways she thought dangerous.

My parents had always hovered over and worried about me, and one of the blessings of our marriage had been Bob's perspective on health matters. He was always there to remind me, if I got sick, that, like everyone – like he did – I'd get better. But the heart surgery had re-opened my fears. For each one I voiced, there were ten about which I kept silent.

108

The trip to the ER for Bob's chest bump, which came on the threshold of our bedtime, was an example. I knew I would not sleep because of my raised anxieties until the matter was settled. Probably Bob knew that too. The explanation we received satisfied us both. Looking at the x-rays, seeing how securely the matrix of wires held together the two sides of Bob's chest, I wished things were as clear about why his weight and blood pressure remained low.

My first call to Hadley, Dr. Volpe's assistant, was about weight-lifting. She okayed my beginning with two-pound dumbbells and inching – or ounce-ing – my way up. And I could carry ten-pounds – which more than covered my gym bag. In two weeks I could do twenty, which meant I needn't embarrassedly trail Adele while she lugged groceries to the car.

I wanted Bob to check with Dr. Fleur before he changed anything. When he'd asked her about lifting weights at his last appointment, she'd said, "Are you crazy?"

He agreed to call her, which pleased me. I understood he wanted to demonstrate his increased wellness to himself and others, but I was worried. Luckily, the "we" component of our relationship was strong enough to bridge these differences and moments of discord. We adjusted for each other. We both wanted this operation to be the last one.

At our December appointment, Dr. Fleur pronounced herself "thrilled." "Your prognosis had been so bad. Now you are like a homemade cake, into which has poured much effort and many ingredients, and now it smells good and tastes good."

My liver enzymes had improved. I could stop the Tramadol. We could stop taking my blood pressure – and could eat out twice-a-week. "It is so satisfying," she said, "to have a patient do what they're supposed to and turn out so well."

We hugged – she and I – then she and Adele.

We left feeling happy, lucky, excited, loved. Dr. Fleur was a good antidote for Dr. Ivanov's "six-months-before-we'll-know." I couldn't rid my mind of his remark, and while only three months had passed, her assessment went a long way toward my believing the result would be good.

I had considered asking Dr. Fleur directly about further surgery but had decided not to. I didn't think I could be reassured totally. But there were many ways Bob could already have had trouble, and he hadn't. His progress was real, and his next echo-cardiogram would be the final piece to the answer.

Then, that weekend, an increase in one of Bob's medications lowered his blood pressure, increased his water retention, and hit him with a fever and chills. The on-call doctor advised that Bob should rest, that I should pamper him (as if I didn't), and that his system would soon adjust to the increased dosage.

That seemed reasonable, but the glow of the appointment had dimmed.

Meanwhile, as a sign of my own recovery, I had returned to Mold Central and, in it, to 2010, before Bob's heart troubles began. One morning I wrote in my journal, "I am often engaged in a battle between the 'moment' and history. Most moments can be endured and dealt with, but once the history they represent floods my mind, I am swept into a torture chamber, where I am trapped, incapable of anything beyond dwelling on the torments that await. I agonize over the latest snag in the house repair process. I must reconstruct our contractor's true nature, my own, and how we interact. My mind cramps, my hands cramp, I want to cry."

It occurred to me that passage captured my relationship to many things, my fears of doctor appointments, my worries about obstacles to Bob's recovery, even everyday matters, like the planning of meals. Every ten days or so, I could become incapable of planning a dinner, feeling I had exhausted all ideas, obsessively running from old stand-by to old stand-by, becoming nauseous in every cell in my body at the overload. In the old days, when this happened, we'd laugh, go out to eat, and the next day I'd be back at the stove; but now, with Bob's options restricted and his health more precarious...

I asked him to solve the problem.

He said, "Let's call Gordie and have whatever he ate."

My brother loved to trumpet his eat-nothing-that-doesn't-stave-off-one-disease-or-another diet. The thought of choosing from a buffet of a hunk of bagel, a yam, and an anti-oxidant puree of spinach, kale and broccoli set us both giggling.

After a concluding "Blech!", I set out for king salmon to set beside oven fries and broiled tomatoes.

I was a month into cardio-rehab when Pam said, "You're the first person since I've been here with zero risk factors, including a Special Forces guy. Isn't that great?"

"But I probably had zero risk factors before my first heart attack," I said.

George, a white-haired epidemiologist on the adjoining recumbent bike, laughed. "Over half the people who have M.I.s had no apparent risk factors."

"Which means," I said, "having no risk factors may be a risk factor."

"But where having taken care of yourself pays off," he said, "is that the survival rate for those who did is much higher than for those who didn't. Plus the 'Did"s have an easier time adjusting their life style to the changes recommended for them."

I thought of gray-complected Malcolm, who left his first session after peddling his bike at a three-year-old's speed, declaring rehab not for him. And Teddy, who weighed twice what I did, yet missed half his sessions. I had been dealt a gene which brought one heart attack and a drug resistance which had brought another. But I had held some aces too.

Nothing guaranteed a transplant's absence from my future; but I meant to focus on what my experiences had taught me. Three times, luck and doctors' skills and God's (or the gods') reconsideration had snatched me from Charon's skiff before it had completed its crossing. I wanted to hold onto that awareness, not because it applied caution's gloomy brake to all I did, but because it had revealed a brightened future was possible. My mind had accumulated seven decades' worth of skepticism and defenses with which to resist this transformation, but I intended to maintain this glimpse of myself as an expanded being.

That afternoon a Volvo tried to screw me out of a parking place. The "Fuck you!" I yelled at the driver, my first expressed anger in a year, felt good too.

Two weeks later, Hadley further eased my restrictions. I could swim and left weights, provided I acted "like it's your first time in a gym." I was forbidden push-ups, pull-ups, or otherwise lifting my body weight. Then Dr. Fleur applied a further brake. I was to stop increasing the weights, once I had reached ten-pounds in each hand. That was fine, since obeying her freed me from having to measure my performance against others at the club. They might have bodily mass on me, but I had increased wisdom.

I wanted to build muscle too. I used two-pounders to do the same routines Bob did with fours, but when I increased to three-, I got sore shoulders and arms.

I did better exercising my lower body. I did intervals on the stationary bike and walked on the treadmill, faster and at higher inclines. It all felt good. I joined Bob in the warm-up and cool-down routines he had learned at rehab. At first, it was so he didn't feel alone, but I came to enjoy it. Manny, an octogenarian jazz pianist, observing from his recumbent bike, said we looked like we were dancing.

We took Saturdays off. That day developed a special feel to it, no place to be, nowhere to go. We'd use some of the time to reacquaint ourselves with our bodies, with hugs and kisses and fondlings. We were patient with each other. While Bob seemed disappointed sometimes when we didn't push on for intercourse, I was relieved to go slowly. I didn't feel ready for more. But anyone who wanted an orgasm got one.

We'd have turkey and avocado sandwiches for dinner, then watch a rented movie. "It's one pleasure after another," one of us would say. We were still short a windowed-door, connecting our dining room to a balcony, the space covered with heavy-duty plastic, but remedying this would have meant a re-engagement with our contractor, for which neither Bob nor I was ready.

One night I dreamt I was trying to find Bob but kept getting lost. We seemed to be in San Francisco, except there were snowstorms. I hitched a ride through the snow to our house. A lesbian came out the front door and shot the car's hub caps off. Her huge dog jumped at me, landed on my head, and could not be pried off. It felt like I was back at California-Pacific, when scary, heavy worries flew up out of nowhere, crashed down, and landed on us.

XVI. GO! GO! GO!

On January 1, 2012, my spirit got an e-mail boost. Benj DeMott, the editor of First of the Month, *an online journal which published an eclectic array of political, social, art, and cultural commentary, including some by Bob, praised chapters of my long-unpublished tennis memoir,* Comeback, *which I had submitted to him months earlier. He especially liked the Roger Federer material and wanted me to make a medley for publication. He also wanted one or two of the other chapters down the line.*

"What a wonderful way to start the New Year!" I said. I felt a jolt of joy and had a gentle cry.

I became eager and able to work. I went through the manuscript, consolidating the Federer and looking for other stand-alone pieces. This allowed me to envision a shorter, tighter book. I found a chapter dealing with my experiences with Breema, a meditative yoga-like practice, which I edited for a shot at The Sun. *Its guidelines said not to expect a response for six-to-nine months. That was okay. The hope of placing my piece there would sustain me.*

The Australian Open, first major of the year, kicked my excitement higher. I no longer had the energy to stay up all night and watch the matches live, so the first days I picked-and-chose with my Internet re-play function and/or recorded and watched on the TV. Bob and I saw Federer's early matches only after knowing the outcome to take the tension down a few notches. I watched his loss to Nadal in the semis alone. Novak Djokovic beat Rafa in just under six hours of brutal play. Cramping and exhausted, they needed to sit on chairs to make it through the awards ceremony. I was almost glad Roger didn't have to be on the other end of that.

But not quite. I was satisfied, though, to have adapted my watching style to again fully enjoy that part of my life.

With the help of Bert, a laid-off Chevron worker, who sold *Street Spirit*, a newspaper distributed by the homeless, whom I'd met outside the French, I moved what I wanted from my office into our basement. Forty years of work compressed into eight storage boxes. Manila folders and paper clips and pens. Squeeze balls promoting physical therapists and post-its that advertised orthopedic surgeons and a rubberized vertebrae which plugged a chiropractor. A century-old, gold-painted brick, a gift from one client. A Thai wall-hanging of a sequined elephant from another. A three-inch-tall brass Buddha from a third.

I propped against a wall diplomas and certificates and framed posters by which I had defined myself to clients and visiting attorneys. One from a rock'n'roll show I had attended in 1956 (Fats Domino, Little Richard, Screamin' Jay Hawkins). Another handed me amidst the tear gas outside the Chicago Hilton in 1968 ("A corrupt convention in a corrupt city"). A hand-lettered cardboard sheet with which the wheelchair-bound wife of a client had panhandled in front of my building ("Thanks to our lawyer we are homeless and without food"). In a competitive market, it had served them well, but she had surrendered it to me, after I tendered a loan. (I'd hung it, framed, behind my desk. "To keep people from getting their expectations too high," I'd explain.)

While in practice, I had liked nearly all my clients. I liked nearly all the other lawyers too. But this world had worn me down. I stood in my basement, as if beside a river, surrounded by alluvial deposits, awaiting leavings yet to come, as it flowed toward the sea.

The day of the office closing, lawyers, secretaries, even the building owners came to say good-bye to Bob. He had been the building's longest tenant and they were sorry to see him go. I salvaged Bob's last to-do list from his desk. It was a page from a note pad, divided into columns, filled with teensy writing, items crossed out as he finished them. It seemed emblematic of his career and good work habits, a treasure to frame and keep. I also inherited a stapler.

We had borrowed Robert's station wagon, and between it and our Honda, we only needed one trip. Bert hefted the boxes and carried them to our cellar, which had been cleared and cleaned for their arrival. I kept him hydrated with orange juice and dusted each of the paintings, posters, art objects, and diplomas, before stacking them for later emplacement.

We paid Bert royally, with gratitude. He went off for a meal, and Bob and I went to the Claremont for a shower. I made chicken soup, with mushrooms, garlic, broccoli florets, and skinny pasta for dinner.

In early February, we had visitors.

When I had first come to Berkeley, I had played weekly pick-up basketball with Artie and three others who had been at Brandeis with us. Ron worked in public relations for Kaiser Permanente. Peter was a public health doctor, who had love beads on his stethoscope and daisies on his VW bug, and Gary... Well, Gary, who'd dropped out junior year, had kept off the grid. In his best scam, using the college transcript of someone with the same name, he'd been admitted to the MA program in theater arts at UC Berkeley, and capitalized on that to be hired as an instructor in drama at an Oakland junior college. Adele and I saw Gary and his then-partner, now-wife Diana a lot. We went to Casa de Eva for tostadas and the Boarding House to hear Jerry Jeff Walker; and, many Saturday nights, in each other's apartments, we watched Bob Newhart and Mary Tyler Moore on TV.

Ron, Artie and I kept playing; but Peter went off to treat refugees in Vietnam, the felasha in Israel, and Native Americans in the southwest; and Gary and Diana moved to southern California. He began writing sitcoms, like the ones we had watched together, and she pursued a PhD in women's studies. Soon he was creating and producing his own shows, and she had written a scholarly book and founded an all-girls private school. They acquired a house in Malibu, then traded it in for homes in Santa Barbara and Vermont and an apartment on Central Park West. (Gary also gave Brandeis $1,000,000, and it gave him an honorary degree.) Early on, they had dropped contact with all of us. Our letters went unanswered, our congratulatory telegrams for his first Emmy ignored. Ron, Artie, even Adele, shrugged. But I felt hurt – and jealous.

Now Gary and Diana, both retired, were returning to Berkeley for an anniversary celebration. They invited Ron and Artie, their wives, Sherry

115

and Sue, and Adele and me to dinner. But first, they hoped for "private time" with the two of us. I was touched, eager – and confused. What, I wondered, was I expecting? One more e-mail correspondent? Respect and admiration for my books? An invitation into their world?

We cleaned the house until it looked like the five-star hotel to which, we assumed, they were accustomed.

I had groaned when I'd heard about Gary and Diana's arrival. Entertaining had become ancient history for Bob and me. But when I saw his excitement, I suggested a tea. When he saw my discomfort, he asked what I needed from him to be comfortable.

We worked together, transforming the house. I'd forgotten how easier chores were with two participants. It was almost fun. Bob wanted to keep at it, after the tea, emptying a cabinet or closet or drawer of its no-longer-needed accumulations each day. That had been the plan for after his retirement, but it had been pre-empted.

Now we put away the sick room paraphernalia, threw out ten years of Consumer Reports and unearthed a lovely oak magazine rack for what was current. We cleared our sun-bright orange couch of its accumulations, remembering that some people found it preferable to lolling on our bed. I felt satisfied we were guest-ready, even with that California King-sized elephant in the middle of the living room. I set out our best dishes, with matching teapot and serving platter.

The afternoon was lovely. My resentments dissolved. Gary said that, when he'd learned from Ron about my heart attacks, he had wanted to fly up immediately. But since I was seeing virtually no one, he had decided to wait. He had arrhythmia himself, for which he was, he assured us, being treated by the best doctors in L.A.; and his concern for me – and the concern I felt for him – seemed genuine and representative of our shared entry into this new dimension of life.

When I expressed my hurt at our severed relationship, he explained, with his old wit and charm – illuminated by new, funny showbiz stories, like a children's book enhanced by illustrations – that he had never felt he had broken contact. But his career had enclosed them in a fishbowl, which, while lavishly furnished, suspended everything outside it as unreal. Now he hosted an annual summer weekend for his high school buddies. He was seeking out old college pals too, and we were an important part of this re-engagement.

I believed he was sincere. I took it as a warming, hopeful part of the healing in progress for us all.

I had lain out on the serving platter scones, butter cookies, and raisin-studded wolverines, along with almonds, walnuts, and hard and soft cheeses. I had filled a cut-glass bowl with sweet cherries. The pot held mint tea.

I had hoped for an afternoon like old times, with the four of us participating as equals. In a larger group, Gary tended to move to center stage and Bob to sink into the shadows. I was glad to hear him express his feelings and to receive Gary's response. I appreciated Gary and Diana's recall of a Thanksgiving we had spent together, in their tiny apartment, shortly after their first daughter had been born. Now they had two, both Harvard graduates, TV writer-producers themselves.

The time passed as I'd wished, relaxed and intimate. We'd all survived health problems, realized some of our hopes, and loved our spouses and lives. We'd grown older, wiser and better.

Days later, on a Valentine's Day walk with Adele, I realized I could "Go! Go! Go!" My breakthrough was not of Jack Kerouac caliber, but I no longer worried about what lay ahead as I stepped from each curb.

"Valentine's Day used to be special," Adele said. "Now every day feels like Valentine's Day." She took my hand. "And I feel more satisfaction and safety and fulfillment and closeness from our marriage than I had ever felt possible."

Nothing felt as good as hearing that.

Sometimes, driving home from workouts, our endorphins humming, we'd exchange happy thoughts. Bob was in a steady state of amazement at how much better he felt. When people asked how he was feeling, he'd answer "Terrific!" We both knew how lucky we were to be doing everything we did.

I woke many mornings feeling the day was a gift. I always told Bob because hearing it made him so happy. One morning, in the car, I said, "I had no idea we would make it through this, or what it would be like if we did. This is beyond my hopes. I always wondered what it would be like to live with a man who smiled. Not that you never smiled, but…"

I asked Bob what his facial expression meant. He said, "Just feeling happy to be with you."

When a patient enters cardio-rehab, the staff sets a METS goal, a measure of his ability to utilize oxygen while exercising. (Everyone requires 3.5 milligrams of oxygen per second, per kilogram of body weight, to keep their organs functioning. So 3.5 mg. equals one MET.) When I began, I had been capable of 3.8 METS. My goal was 5.6. Two weeks before graduation, I had reached 6.3. "Bob has had excellent improvement in aerobic exercise capacity," my final evaluative report said.

It read a bit like "Plays well with others" – but was, I recognized, more significant.

Nurse after nurse complimented me on how well I had done. They would be sorry to see me go. I was sorry too. They had been encouraging and kind, and they had saved my life – literally.

Each person's completion of the program was announced. Everyone applauded. Cupcakes were served. After my last bite, I took a long look at the bench on which I'd lain eleven months before. The rehab sessions had become so stitched into our week it would take a while, without the support and monitoring, to embrace our new freedom.

The next time to be anxious was the echo-cardiogram, which Dr. Fleur had ordered for my March appointment. She had said, "What is important is how you feel and what you can do, all of which is great, not what the test will show." But I viewed anything that might read negatively as a threat. I tuned out the tech's conversation and did not look at the numbers on the screen.

The night before Dr. Fleur was to review the results with us, I dreamed I was playing right field for the New York Yankees in Game Seven of the World Series. I had been out of action a year. My swing could not catch up to a fastball, and line drives were too quickly upon me. I told Ralph Houk, "For the good of the team, skip, take me out." Massaging me between innings, he flipped open a bone in my chest like it was hinged.

No matter how far I'd come, I thought, the world could undo me any moment.

But Dr. Fleur was glowing.

My ejection fraction, while just 35 percent was actually better than the previous higher readings. Because the surgery had repaired my leaky valve, she explained, my heart was handling a much greater blood flow. My pre-surgery heart had only pumped one-third to one-half of what it was pumping now. So even though the percentage of blood being expelled was less, the amount of blood circulating to feed my body and mind was greater. Plus, there was no longer any "regurgitation." When I was tested next, the flow might be better still.

I could stop blowing into the device to build my lung capacity. I could cut my Lexapro in half. I could stop my antacid and sleeping pills entirely.

Oh, if the EF did not improve, I might need a pacemaker, but that was "unlikely."

"I'll see you in six months," she said. "Then we may go to annual appointments."

"But I'll miss you," I blurted out. "Can we have lunch?"

On my walk to the French the next morning, I spoke aloud to my mother and father. "I feel great," I said. "I've never been happier."

Three days later, I received word, like an appointment reminder, that Peter, the public health physician, had died from lung cancer.

XVII. SHOOT HIM

I was working to construct a life – or, rather, remodel the one I'd had on the frame which stood.

Each morning, after breakfast and a half-dozen pills, I went to the French. I ordered my short double, took my table, and observed this world. The French had its evening crowd, its afternoon crowd, and its morning crowd, of which I was now part.

We were primarily elderly. We were an anesthesiologist, cartoonist, contractor (two), fine artists (several), folk musicians (several more), high school teacher, mathematician, mime (retired), photographers (several), plumber, poet, professor emeritus (anthropology), river rafting guide (retired), roadie (formerly with the Allman Brothers, now homeless), union organizer, yoga instructor. We had come from Brazil, Bulgaria, Ethiopia (or Eritrea), Israel, Poland, Syria. Robert Reich was followed through the front door by an obese woman, with matted hair, bare midriff, and in flip-flops.

The French was a social café. Its two rooms, larger in front, smaller in back, held only two electrical outlets, which deterred the roosting of the silent, studious lap-top dependent.) The chatter level – politics and weather, health and films – dissuaded attempts at chess or go. Groups as large as twenty congregated. Others confined themselves to trios or quartets. A minority, like me, customarily solo-ed. We learned each other's schedules and habits. If our favorite tables were taken, we knew upon whom to keep an eye, and when to grab up our cups and saucers and pounce.

I made acquaintances as easily as I wanted. I discussed heart attacks with Harry and Ann. I advised Steve and Sulu on workers' comp. Hap complimented my black leather pants. Joey invited me to the off-the-books concerts he hosted in his converted laundry-house. I swapped Liz a book I'd written for a t-shirt she'd designed. (In a room of odd, brightly colored creatures, a grey-shaded, nerdy fellow stood alone. "Bob," it said, "is a strange bird.")

Mainly, I wrote. In the first half of 2012, I finished short pieces on Flannery O'Connor, *Ed the Happy Clown*, *The King of Marvin Gardens*, my experiences at the 1960 Democratic Convention, and my most recent cardiovascular adventures. After I finished one project, I immediately took up the next. My writing filled my head. Where I once worried over checks to and medical treatment for clients, I now rearranged words within sentences and sentences within paragraphs. I did this as I sat or drove or showered. I was not certain this was a good thing, but I figured a head had to hold something.

After Bob came back from the French, he and I went to the Claremont. Three days a week, he did the consecutive ten-minute stints he'd done in rehab on machines equivalent to those he'd used there. Three days, he worked out with light weights and either walked solo near our house or with Robert in Tilden Park. I used similar machines at the club, or swam, or walked by myself. We had been told to allow a day a week for Bob's body to recover, or we'd have filled a seventh.

One Saturday, while on the treadmill, I watched the semi-final match from Indian Wells, between John Isner and Novak Djokovic, rooting for Isner, thinking he would be easier for Roger to beat in the final. I jogged faster and faster as the match went on; and when Isner won, let out a "WHOOP!" and punched the air. Next thing I knew, I'd flow off the treadmill and landed – SMACK – on my back.

I was in excruciating pain. I was conscious but afraid to move. I realized Bob was so focused on his workout, he didn't know I'd fallen. Two doctors came to my aid. They placed a towel pillow under my head and checked my arms and legs. I had no broken bones. My neck had been strong enough to keep my head from banging on the floor. They had me sit up before attempting to stand. I asked one to tell Bob I was okay. I was terrified what the shock of seeing me on the floor might have on him. But he held steady, and I was glad to have him join me.

I stood and took a couple steps. It hurt to breath. One of the doctors said I had bruised, maybe broken, a rib and spasmed my upper back, and that the pain would be intense for a few days. I could go home, ice, and take Ibuprofen. I was relieved I didn't need the hospital. We had had enough of them. Still, the swiftness with which I'd gone from okay to hurt was unsettling.

The cardio-machines were in one room and the bar bells, press benches, and TechnoGym equipment in another. But I lifted weights in a different building, one which was home to the aerobics studio and Pilates machines. The weights there ranged from one to fifty pounds, so I did not feel diminished by – and was not tempted to compete with – people grunting, sweating, hoisting their way through bigger numbers. That some of those working with poundage beyond me, even here, were women, did not disturb me. Acceptance, I reminded myself, was a good thing. As I progressed, from five-pound weights, to six, to seven, I recalled when I could not lift the orange juice from the refrigerator. I remembered when my skin strung slack and grey over bone.

In the room where I lifted, personal trainers massaged clients, corrected their Downward Facing Dogs, ran them through TRX drills. The more martial had trainees punch and kick a heavy bag. I kept an eye on them. The THWACK when a blow landed tempted like a six-foot apple. I went on line: "How to throw a jab?" I asked. "How to throw a hook?" I took notes about foot placement, hip rotation, and angle of arm at impact. I studied myself in full-length mirrors. (Why, I wondered, is this man smiling?) I watched You Tube videos of Sugar Ray and The Brown Bomber. Bob Foster, a light-heavyweight champion – tall and thin, like me – carried his left low, so I decided I would.

I found a pair of unpadded, leather-and-mesh weight-lifting gloves in the bottom of my locker. They covered the palms and striking knuckles but left the fingers free. They sounded good against the bag but afforded scant protection. (Hands, I knew, broke easier than heads.) Then David, a friend who'd sparred in East Bay gyms, loaned me sixteen-ounce, lace-up Everlasts. ("Great gloves!" the most militant of the trainers said. "They don't make them like that anymore.") I felt ready to rumble.

I hit the bag on weight days. I had the jab. I added a right cross. My left hook, however, disgraced my Joe Frazier/Lennie Mathews/Bennie Brisco Philadelphia roots, and my uppercuts threatened to fracture my wrists. (Those, I stopped, after David counseled that landing them on a heavy bag would, at least, sprain something.) Still, the process offered the possibility of, if not mastery, improvement. At my age, this seemed something. What was more, given the oddball unlikelihood of the endeavor, it was a kick. (My last effort at boxing had ended with a whipping, in day camp, in 1951, by a boy both younger and shorter.) My smile broadened; the bounce to my step increased with each outing. As I had learned to craft sentences that resonated, I crafted punches that THWACK-ed. Do that enough, I reasoned, with pace and rhythm, and you will have beauty. The bag even allowed for rage. In each sharply expelled breath and snapping blow, I struck against a friend's malignant tumor, or damaged frontal lobe, or my own stent-dependent arteries. "Take that, Fate, you bastard!"

Dr. Fleur said I could hit anything that did not hit back. When the Claremont denied my request for a speed bag ("Too noisy"), I installed one in my basement.

"Excellent for hand-eye co-ordination," the trainer said.

"Great," I said. "That'll make getting my pills into my mouth easier."

Joyce Carol Oates has written "that life is a metaphor for boxing... you and your opponent so exactly matched it's impossible not to see that your opponent is you." Defend yourself at all times, she instructs, for you rarely see the blow that fells you. When someone has been dropped, I saw, whether by an incoming right cross or his own body's short-coming, the challenge is to rise, shake off the cobwebs, and resume the contest.

I wondered if the Maccabiah Games had events for super-seniors. At 6'3", I could be a middleweight contender.

On days Bob boxed, I walked, finishing off with a few light weight exercises myself. I included some I'd learned rehabbing a meniscus I'd torn playing tennis years before. I had the idea of returning to the court. A couple times I found an empty one and ran around without a racquet. It was fun and highly aerobic, or anaerobic, or both.

Bob looked beautiful, dancing around the punching bag. I admired his resolve and shared his pleasure as his muscles filled out. He made friends in that room, as he had in the café. His ease with people seemed to have grown exponentially. I used to be like that. It almost felt we had switched places.

Gary forwarded the e-mail addresses of two Brandeis friends with whom he'd renewed contact. I wrote both, received replies, and, from each connection, felt strengthened. When another friend's mother passed, I called with condolences. When the wife of a fellow at the French died, I offered sympathy. When an attorney who had become close to my parents died, I sent his widow a card. When a memorial service was held at the French for a fellow I knew only by sight, I attended. Two years before, I thought, none of this would have stirred me to these actions.

I would have liked more erections than my medications allowed, but… My fitness astounded me. The community of the French engaged me. My writing pleased me. My capacity to feel for and respond to others warmed me.

We met with an estate planner in a lake front, high rise office building in Oakland. Bob had earned enough. We had not spent too much. Our financial situation was solid. Still, we took no action. This was more from inertia than confidence.

There were questions we could – or would – not answer. Who would be our executor? We had no children. We had no relatives within 400 miles. Our friends were our age or older. To whom would we give our money if we had any left? To what charities? Who would inherit what jewelry and other objects of value? I suddenly understood the difficulty that made my mother start asking us, when young, what pieces we liked.

It had made no difference though. Somehow, none of us received our favorites.

Dr. Fleur ordered a carotid artery scan to cover one more base. I had narrowing, right and left, but overall it read fine.

Two weeks before the September appointment with Dr. Fleur, I had another echo.I told the tech I did not want to know what it showed.

"Understood."

Twenty minutes into it, she said, "Perfect" – and paused – "Oh, that's right. You didn't want to know."

I smiled.

Later, she said, "Amazing, what they can do."

I smiled more.

I felt confident. I didn't want a pacemaker. I didn't want anything. I'd had enough. I preferred believing I was a normal person, albeit one with a lot of metal in him.

"You are going to have to shoot him," Dr. Fleur told Adele.

My BNP was now in the 200s. My EF was 48.9. Almost all my heart's swelling was gone. It had dead places, sure, but it did all it was supposed to. This was, to Dr. Fleur, "like, *Yes!* If all my patients were like this," she said, "I would be famous world-wide."

Aside from cutting back from two-baby-aspirin-a-day to one, I need change nothing. I was to return in eight months, our longest separation yet. "Celebrate," Dr. Fleur said. "Eat sushi. But watch the soy sauce."

I might really have twenty years. For the first time since this saga had begun, I did not have a test waiting to worry me. Dr. Fleur had said I knew what pains to be concerned about, so the rest of them I wouldn't.

When Dr. Fleur said, "Shoot him," we laughed, but I never could have made a joke of what had been a constant fear, Bob's death.

XVIII. 86,397 IS NOT ENOUGH

On October 13th, I fell, crumpled really, consciousness lost, bounced from the canvas before the count hit "Three," bleeding from the head and leg.

I had risen from the bed and crossed the room to shelve a book. "Got up too quick," I told Adele. I promised not to do that again. (Sure, I thought.) In the corner, near where I landed was a sharply cornered end table. If I had struck my temple…

"At least we know your blood thinner works," she said.

I had seen Bob's feet go out from under him. I was off the bed as he hit the floor, whacking his head and body against the cabinet that the TV rested on. But I couldn't stop any of it.

I held Bob as he made it back to the bed. I got disinfectant, a clean towel, ice packs, Ibuprofen and cared for his wounds. I remembered the second and near fatal heart attack and how, for the longest time, I'd blamed myself for not having been with him, thinking it might not have happened, invoking Heisenberg's observer-effects-events at a quantum level as a metaphor for the power of loving presence. The complications of such an analogy when applied to the human heart popped up and scared me.

I wished that I had said, "You've gotten up too fast" before he'd moved forward. The hell if it annoyed him.

We believed the fall had been a vaso-vagal response, where a sudden drop in blood pressure causes a lack of blood flow to the brain. Being tall, making the blood's trip longer, and being on beta blockers, I was particularly at risk. We were even more – if semi-humorously – concerned because we had tickets for a Bob Dylan concert, at UC's outdoor Greek Theater, for which we'd planned a re-engagement with our roots by smoking pot. Given my collapse, we ran this plan by Dr. Fleur. "Take no more than two tokes," she said, "and be careful when you stand to cheer."

The evening of the show was cold and overcast. On our left sat two twenty-something Asian-American women from San Jose. Adele and I had been hearing Dylan, live, for nearly fifty years; and as we often did with people much younger than us, we asked what had brought them.

They explained that the brother of one, who was boyfriend of the other, had introduced them to Dylan on weekends they spent on the run from alcoholic parents. Since the fellow's surprise death, six months before, they had been saving money for the concert, knowing he would have been there. In fact, they believed he was. Each had brought his photograph to contemplate, while they smoked the joints through which the music reached them. It occurred to me that, at their age, an equivalent would have been our driving an hour to seek transcendence from the music of someone who had first hit the charts before the U.S. had entered World War I.

I silently wished the young women luck. I hoped for the young man's presence. It did not occur to me to think that Peter, who was also a Bob Dylan fan, might be there too.

As the sun set, the clash of last sunbeams and stage lights formed a rainbow necklace, seeming to emanate from Dylan up to the stars and out to us. As that faded, the stage turned golden, with strands of light reaching from him to the heavens and back. It felt a cradle of goodness in which he rocked us.

That Bob was well enough to be there, and to have his two tokes, seemed as magical as what the women beside us had sought. We exchanged stories, back and forth, in which Bob's heart played a large part of what we offered. They were younger than Bob and I had been on our first date, when, hearing Pete Seeger sing "Blowin' in the Wind" and "A Hard Rain's A-Gonna Fall," we had begun a lifelong love affair, both with each other and with Dylan.

Our seat-mates were as excited for us being there as for themselves, and I believed the brother would be there for them, even before my toke. We were all together, forever young.

On Thanksgiving, Adele showed me photos she had taken on her phone when I was ill but had concealed from me until now. I was shocked by how ravaged I appeared.

I scanned my life. I considered twists and turns and "what-ifs." I considered who I had been, who I had become, and what had affected me how. Via e-mail, I reached out to people I'd played football with in high school and others with whom I'd hung with in bars during law school, as if their clues would unearth a last page on which mysteries would be solved. The most startling news to reach me was of Lester and Edward, two Negroes on the periphery of my adolescent social crowd. Edward, who played bass, went to high school with Davie Peters, whom I had known since elementary school, and Lester went to another with Max Garden, whom I had known longer. Edward and Lester were jazz musicians. They rarely had gigs and, if they did, the gigs rarely paid; but that is who they were and that is what they did. If Max or Davie or I had a car, we gave Edward and his bass a ride to his rehearsal, and if you had a piano for Lester, that rehearsal might be in your living room.

It was Lester who, through Robitussin AC, became the first druggie I knew. And it was Edward who, when asked if he was going to college, uttered the weighty line I fed to a minor character in my first novel, "What, man, you mean be a everybody?" But, in 1976, it had been Davie who suicided with pills and, a dozen years later, it had been Max who died of an infection secondary to intravenous drug use. If you had told me in 1960 that Edward and Lester would outlive Max and Davie...

Edward replied by e-mail.

Lester called. "Is this Spruce Hill Bob?"

My heart filled. It seemed the tides of time could reveal unexpected treasures buried beneath the beach.

I admired Bob's impulse to reconnect with friends. He had become able to view his past with new understanding, and to offer forgiveness to others for hurts received – and to himself for hurts given. I'd had opportunities to do the same but either hadn't tried or tried and it had not worked.

My Brandeis roommate, Shoshana, was a brilliant student. I wanted to be like her. I changed majors to psychology and studied like she did. My grades improved, then soared. While I could not match her affairs with married professors, I was popular and told a good story. When I came to San Francisco, she drove with me in my tangerine Opel. We hiked and lay on the beach at Lake Tahoe and took dips in its icy water. At night, we went to Harvey's Resort Casino, dressed like high class hookers in sexy silk sheaths, slit up one side, and picked up two octogenarians who wined and dined us, before we ditched them. Mine was deaf. He kept eating off my plate. I'd say, "Hey, that's mine!" But he finished my baked potato, sour cream and chives. We only ate one meal a day to save money, and I'd really wanted it.

Shoshana returned to Boston and medical school, and I settled into my new life at S.F. State. I thought we'd be friends forever, but, by April, our correspondence had petered out. I had new friends and could not cope with her continually picking up men who abused her. These rituals made me feel angry and sad and powerless to help. When I asked her not to tell me about any more debaucheries, her letters stopped. When I learned she had graduated at the top of her class, married a successful architect, and had a child. She seemed way ahead of me, stuck as I was, writing an impossible paper on Samuel Beckett's novels and veteran of my own not-so-good relationships.

After Bob came out, we made a trip to New York where we met with Shoshana. We had a good time, but our lives continued without contact, until our fifteenth college reunion. Shoshana was first on the "Will Attend" list, and I traipsed around with her to talk with everyone we had known. A pattern developed. She'd say, "You remember Adele?" No one did. I sat alone, wondering how much of my memory of college was my own and how much the vicarious thrill I took from an incorporation of her more adventurous life.

So connections felt too hard for me. New friendships, or revived old ones, meant more invitations, more intrusions, more people's health to worry about, and more funerals to go to. We lived with the phone turned off, a broken buzzer at the front door, our alarm on and locks secured. Bob had room for more, but I didn't. It sounded to others like I was nuts; but, to me, it smelled like freedom.

I treasured the memory of each person I had been close to, the experiences we'd shared, from grade school through graduate school, and whatever eventually drove us apart. The same went for my working years, as a mental health professional, teacher at an alternative high school, Xerox operator, and coffee maker at the original Peet's. But I had enough for now.

Out of the pleasant blue, an e-mail from Diana landed. Gary had been rushed to Columbia Hospital in Manhattan complaining of headaches. After undergoing surgery for a "mass" on his brain, he had been released to their apartment on Central Park West. The next step was a consultation at Duke Medical Center. The finest doctors were again on his case, she reassured.

The words of love and caring with which I replied did not dispel the cloud above me. Its shadow tested the limits of my optimism and waved raw meat before the snapping jaws of fear. I recalled advise from my mother, when Adele had a melanoma scare, thirteen years before. "Hope you're lucky. Hope your doctors know what they're doing. And consider converting to Roman Catholicism." I dreamed Diana and Gary, Adele and I were chased through an old house by an axe-wielding maniac.

My second fall came in mid-December. While coming up from the locker room at the Claremont, my toes caught on the lip of a step and dropped me on both knees. I put it down to my thoughts having been elsewhere. My difficulty rising, though, brought the attentions of others. I refused the aid of a woman who, rushing to me, said, "I'm a physician."

I sat in the TV room while a football game showed. I was no longer "Boy-am-I-in-good-shape!" I had seen old men fall in locker rooms. Now I seemed to have become one.

Someone called to Adele while she was drying off from the shower. She arrived, hastily dressed and dripping.

A third knockdown can stop the fight. Mine came one week into 2013. Again, I had risen from the bed. This time, I was two steps into the kitchen when I collapsed. I had a cut lip, bloodied nose, and a mouse under one eye. Adele ran from her study, having heard the thud. She sat on the floor beside me, while I reconstructed what had happened. She brought me ice packs and a chair. She helped me rise and sit, until I was ready to walk to the bathroom, where she washed and disinfected my wounds.

Dr. Fleur put me on a twenty-four hour heart monitor, with a blood test and stress-echo to follow. She told me to arise slowly and avoid prolonged standing. She remained ninety-nine percent certain it was vagal, but...

The good news was she certified my disabled parking placard as "Permanent."

The combined traumas of Bob's falls and Gary's bad news had escalated my anxieties, preoccupations, and obsessive thoughts to a degree I could not bear. I felt shaken to my roots, as if by a series of 6.0 earthquakes, and left permanently wobbly. My panics trebled in numbers and intensity. It occurred to me we were out of parents. We, our siblings and friends were the next forest to be decimated. I began anti-depressants.

I'd been on the verge for years. Sometimes the battle between the pros and cons was itself enough to lift me out of a funk. I had piled up reasons to try. Marilyn knew people who'd suffered from writer's block but on medication became able to produce at a fast clip. The mother of a woman at the club had used them and found a new lover. Other people had managed their lives better in more conventional ways. Bob's reaction to his Lexapro offered, first hand, the best of reasons to try.

But I feared not having my own mind. Its problems notwithstanding, I liked it and what it produced; and I feared it would flatten out, and I'd lose my creativity. Each moment of Bob's progress provided a breather from my malaise, and the hours we spent together at the gym or on the bed kept me afloat; but, alone or awake during the night, I was tortured by thoughts of even more difficult health scenarios than the ones we had survived. I squandered the hours

Bob spent at the café by watching Lifetime movies. I felt guilty but needed those hours of obliteration. Terror worked best; films that made me cry second. I needed stronger and stronger doses to get a breather from my own self-inflictions.

What made it worse was that everyone else was celebrating Bob's recovery. They were happy for us, individually and collectively, and I felt wretched and isolated in my misery. It reminded me of the Woody Allen film, where two trains pass, going in opposite directions, one full of people laughing and full of life. Bob, filled with his energies, was on that train. I was on the other, isolated from the celebration, one of the sad and old, sitting glumly alone, depleted and exhausted.

I could not bear it. I didn't care what kind of mind I was left with, as long as I no longer suffered. My internist wrote me a prescription for Lexapro, which I immediately filled. The dose she prescribed led to more anxiety, so I halved, then quartered it. By the time I saw her two weeks later, I had made it back to the starting point. I felt more in control and, over-all, better, a state which, I knew, exceeded the actual possible benefits of the medication since it took six weeks to take effect. But I didn't care why I felt better. What was important was that I did. I was tolerating the dose and could raise it in tiny increments as I chose and feel better yet. I was giddy with hope.

We saw Dr. Fleur a month later.

"We have to talk," she said, when she called us from the waiting room. Adele and I looked at each other.

I felt great. I had not fallen again. I had crushed the stress-echo, my heart rate hitting 149 beats per minute, ninety-nine percent of normal. My ejection fraction was a still-stunning 48.8. And the monitor had shown no arrhythmia, with my heart beating between forty-three times a minute, when I slept, and 103, when I exercised. But for 3.2 consecutive seconds, out of the day's 86,400, my heart had not beat at all.

You would think a 99.99997% success rate would be fine. But skip another second or two – BANG! – you are gone!

It could be an anomaly. It might never happen again. But Dr. Fleur was recommending an Internal Cardiac Defibrillator (ICD). It would be simple, she said. A slit in the chest. The connection of one lead to the right ventricle and one to the right atrium. One night in the hospital. Pain for a week. I should not raise my left arm overhead or lift over ten-pounds for a month. No cell phones in my breast pocket or going through metal detectors forever. Keep away from large magnets – or was it large mammals? I was too wobbly by then to be sure.

The stents after my first M.I. had taken four hours, instead of the predicted one. The second M.I. had me in a coma for two days. The repair of my mitral valve had triggered uncontrollable bleeding. Adele and I loved Dr. Fleur. We felt blessed that I was walking and talking. But if we never saw another hospital...

Dr. Fleur explained. The heart functioned through the steady pulsing of electrical impulses. The aging of the dead and damaged portions of mine would increase the chance of its misfiring – and my risk of sudden cardiac arrest. "I've given this a lot of thought," she said. "We should proceed while you are strong and fit."

"We've already nominated you for sainthood," Adele said. "We figure, with Bob as your first miracle, you only need one more. We will do whatever you say."

XIX. NOTHING LEFT

A few days later Dr. Fleur called. Dr. Chi the "electrician" of her group, would operate. "I told him 'Don't mess around. He's going to make me a saint, and I want to be one.'" The operation was scheduled in two weeks. Then a secretary informed us that he hospital did not have an anesthesiologist available then. Call me a pussy, but I preferred one. The operation was delayed – and landed on my birthday.

I was cool with that. I figured God less likely to fuck with me then. (It felt safer, like having nuns in line when boarding a plane.) "You'll never get a more expensive present," the secretary said.

Dr. Chi sounded young and energetic. But the operation would have one wrinkle. Some installations take an hour; mine would last three. I had rehabbed my heart so well that Medicare would not automatically cover the cost. He would have to authenticate my need by running a catheter up through my femoral artery and stimulating a life-threatening fibrillation.

When I told Budd, he explained, "The government doesn't mind sticking a $100,000 gizmo in the chest of some homeless junkie, who'd just soon rip it out and pawn it, but it won't let your doctor decide what's best for you."

"What if my heart won't cooperate into misbehaving?" I said.

"Don't worry. We docs've learned to be devious."

I must have looked doubtful.

"Physician-to-physician," Budd said, "I approve everything Dr. Fleur's doing. She has much invested in you and weighed the risks of the procedure versus the danger of ignoring the findings and acted appropriately."

"Well, I don't want to do anything that would make her feel bad."

A few nights before I was to go in, I dreamt Adele and I had bought a store in San Francisco's Mission District. In one of our first days there, I returned from the bank and could not find it. I walked back and forth, checking each storefront. Then I recognized that the portion of the block where it had been contained only rubble. A passer-by explained the site had exploded. Police and firemen and ambulance crews had come and gone. Nothing was left. No one remained.

I could not believe it. I expected to spot Adele's yellow, ankle length rain slicker in the crowd. But she was not there. The only Adele was an image which materialized to tell me she was not in the hospital either. As the news sunk in, I lay face down and licked the sidewalk as if to absorb some remnant of her.

I awoke, terrified.

"Bob!" Adele called. She was already awake, terrified by her own dreams.

The news of the operation had flooded my mind with memories of old hospital experiences. But my anti-depressant kept me from a full-blown panic. I was grateful for the modicum of control over my thoughts.

The operation went so smoothly, and Bob's heart proved so easy to fibrillate – hitting 233 beats a minute – Dr. Chi threw in some fix-up work while he was in there. Bob was walking before dinner and home the next day. Incision care was a breeze compared with his other surgeries.

We had good news from Diana too. The consultant at Duke had prescribed thirty radiation sessions for Gary and over three-dozen pills a day, but his MRI looked fine. We e-mailed he was up for Comeback Player of the Year. She replied that we should think of Bob's defibrillator as his heart's conscience.

The pain was no problem. I was off Tylenol in two days. Not being able to lift weights was annoying, but I was on the cardio machines full bore within the week. My biggest problem was the ICD's visibility. I was so thin, it looked like someone had sewn a pocket watch inside my chest. "No more walking around in tight Angora sweaters," I said.

"You'll get used to it," Adele said.

"Maybe I need another for balance."

"A tattoo would be simpler."

This vanity bothered me. But I felt officially transformed into an *alte cocker*, from the vital, vigorous twenty-nine-year-old I still half-held myself to be. I thought the clothing cops would confiscate my black leathers and order me into white loafers, lemon cardigans, and lime polyester slacks pulled above my navel. In the locker room, I kept a shirt on till the last second and cast a towel over my shoulder to and from the shower. It used to be that I rooted, sportswise, for Philadelphians, then Jews, then bald guys. Now when the NCAA basketball finals kicked off, I backed Iowa State because its coach came accessorized like me. Was this jobbie really necessary, I wondered.

My next appointment with Dr. Fleur changed that.

One factor was her happiness. She seemed to feel I was protected at last. Registering the concern lifted from her lifted some from Adele and me. Another was that after I confessed my self-consciousness, she told of a vital, vigorous, forty-year-old patient who'd refused one. She went – BANG! – on her morning jog.

Then there were the ICD's wonders. If the battery was low, or a lead was loose, it would beep. at a time of day of my selection, to warn me. (If I missed the signal, it would beep at that time every day, until I reacted.) If my heart beat off-rhythm or slower or faster than Dr. Fleur wanted, the ICD would choose from a range of pulses and jolts to correct it. "Think of it as having a built-in paramedic, who can reach the scene, diagnose the problem, and fix it – within twenty seconds," her medical assistant said, as she customized my settings. And throughout the day, the ICD would collect information on my heart's function, which it would transmit, over the phone, while I slept, to the office, so I need not go there.

"This is it," Dr. Fleur said. "You're done. Modern medicine has nothing left to put in you."

It left me a-tremble. I recognized that in a few years even this technology might seem Paleolithic. I understood that op-ed pages could be filled debating whether taxpayers ought to keep me sniffing, instead of fertilizing, roses. But with clear conscience, bouncing step, hip-riding jeans, and engineer boots, I went forth. And the next morning at the café, when Liz asked how I was doing, I whipped up my t-shirt to show her.

Dr. Fleur's excitement amped up my feeling that I could get better too.

That night I dreamt I was a member of a group of writers who could not understand each other's points of view, like a multiple, whose different personalities aren't privy to each other. Then I realized that if I listened closely, I could understand each one. I woke up with a smile.

When I brushed my teeth and looked in the mirror, I felt pretty. It recalled to me my euphoria, some thirty-eight-years earlier, when, following an allergic reaction that had required a period of steroid use, my whole mind opened wide making every moment a jewel. My senses had become sharp and overlapped, a phenomenon known as synesthesia. There had been no boundaries between me and how other people felt. I had near photographic memory of the happenings of each day, and almost no need for sleep or food. I had occasional frightening moments, but the thought of losing this gift of perception, like looking down and not knowing my feet were feet, overrode any wish to be sedated. Some people thought I was insane, but my doctor told me that this was the way life and the mind were meant to be.

Sometimes, in the midst of our ordeal, I'd wished my euphoria would return. This happy moment was not it, but it was the best I'd felt in a long time. I hoped Bob's continued recovery and my anti-depressants would take me someplace near my mind's potential for joy and wonder again.

CODA (Bob)

I don't necessarily agree with Nietzsche that what doesn't kill us makes us stronger. But it can alter who we are and how we behave in the world.

The prevailing wisdom used to be that individual personalities became fixed by early adulthood. Then neuroscientists discovered the default-mode network, a region of the brain which held it together, like a conductor directing an orchestra, becoming, in effect, one's ego, or self. Later, scientists learned that certain stimulants, like psilocybin, could loosen this network's grip on things. Maybe something like that happened with me. Or maybe, after I closed my law practice, the channels of my brain, which I had filled worrying whether I should do this or that, had filled with something else, like enjoying the orange and yellow flashing on the inside of my eyelids when I meditated, or the tops of trees swaying in the wind as I walked down Spruce Street toward the French.

Anyway, I had become a different person.

For one thing, I didn't swim anymore.

Oh, I might do a few laps on a hot day; but as a cardiovascular exercise, it was out. I absolutely believed swimming had not caused my first heart attack, but I felt more comfortable on land. And when I did laps, after each, I hung on the edge of the pool for extra seconds, checking all systems, before setting out for the other end.

I checked all chest pains too. Where was it located exactly? What was it like? How did it compare to those I'd had before? Usually, within minutes, I chucked them aside. Records of my doctors' visits consistently recorded my reports of "No chest discomfort or ischemia." Oh, I had "SOB" climbing hills or "dizziness" exiting the car, but I was "doing fine," "feeling great," and "happy." My meds were tweaked, up or down, on or off; but my weight (165-70), pulse (50-60), blood pressure (100-110), and ejection fraction (45-48.5) remained reassuringly consistent.

Only one chest pain, which had come on after I'd been wrestling with a new computer for twenty minutes, was different enough to set me and Adele to Alta Bates. The pain was gone by the time Dr. Galloway, who happened to be on-call, saw me; but a blood panel's measurement of my heart's contraction rate caused him concern.

He had an ambulance transport me to Summit for an angiogram. My right femoral artery didn't allow access – too much past traffic, I presumed – so he used my left and found blockage in my LAD. Perhaps my medications had caused a closure. Perhaps scar tissue had done it. Perhaps some other "artifact" was involved. Maybe two stents had slipped out of alignment. Whatever it was, he cleared it with a balloon.

I was released the next morning. "Very nothing," Dr. Fleur assessed a few days later. My vessels were clear. No damage had occurred. I could return to all activities.

Friends changed too.
Some got new hips.
Some new knees
Some got grandchildren.
One or two hit the trifecta.
Everyone weathered everything. That seemed the way, most of the time, it was.

Gary was one of the other times.
He became too weak to walk or rise. An MRI confirmed his tumor's growth. He was in ICU a month. When he returned to their apartment, he spent most of his time sitting on its balcony, holding Diana's hand, while his granddaughters picked flowers for him in the garden below.

He passed on June 22, 2013. I thought about past times. I thought about times that couldn't be. I thought it could have been Adele and me. It was a blessing that it wasn't. It was cruel – for others – that this was so.

I hit and hit the heavy bag.

I died myself, August 31. Well, not exactly.

I knew I was dead because the times I had almost died, lying unconscious on operating tables while "Code"s were called about me, had not been like this, which could only mean I had passed beyond "almost" and reached "entirely." On my own bed. In my own living room.

The big difference was that I had left my body. I – my "self" – hovered above it, trying to re-enter and resume life. Once I nearly did, but then I slipped away and headed from the living room toward the next stage, where people who had already passed, my parents, my sister, friends, awaited. Adele was trying to get me to return to my body, to not leave her. But it was too late. This time I had gone too far.

I had blown out my heart. It was entirely my fault. I felt terrible. I was gripped by the crushing squeeze of regrets. Things undone. Things unsaid. The loss of me which would rip Adele apart.

On the other hand, it was not that bad. My gone-from-my-body self was aware of everything that was occurring in the living room. Adele just wasn't aware of me. And she didn't know that, when she passed from this life into the stage I'd reached, we would be together. So she felt terrible and, since this was my fault, I felt terrible too.

But let me back up.

My new life had included regularly smoking dope. Dr. Zipp had written me a prescription; and the legalized pot world, with its dispensaries offering senior discounts, free samples and reward cards, was a kick to someone who had last been a "head" when the fuzz could come busting down your door any moment. After expressing my delight over this cultural progress at the French, I began receiving gifts from those already familiar with it. One had been homemade brownies. But I had forgotten how many their baker had said to eat and doubled the recommended portion.

Adele had not been in the living room when I had died. Nor had she been urging me not to leave her. She had been gone only a few minutes and, when she returned, had seen I was in trouble. Should she call someone?

Good idea.

A few minutes later – six, or eight, or a dozen beefy para-medics filled the room. The tattooed, shaved-headed crew chief hooked me to an EKG. My vital signs were – amazingly, comfortingly – normal.

We told him about the brownies. I did not sense this information would reach my FBI file. I was not asked to give up my dealer's name. In fact, I seemed to have been instantly transformed from an object of concern into one of amusement. I was relieved at not being dead. But I was embarrassed at being this old hippie who could not handle his dope, a joke to be told whenever ambulance crews gathered.

When I noticed the living room empty, I hopefully asked Adele if I had hallucinated the paramedics too.

I would have liked to report my insights into the afterlife with conviction. I would have liked this, even if I hadn't known of the six-figure book advance paid to that seven-year-old boy for his account of his in-the-beyond meeting with Jesus.

But, Dr. Fleur explained, patients undergoing surgery often partially regain consciousness and find themselves disoriented, frightened, as their sedation wears off. She thought, with the dope, I had retrieved and replayed thoughts I had during such times but which I had repressed, and that it might benefit my brain to have rid itself of this load. There was enough of a familiarity to the thoughts I'd had, as to a tune heard, forgotten, and later re-encountered, that this seemed persuasive to me. Popular culture, like the TV detective shouting to his shot and fallen partner "Stay with me!" seemed to have imprinted itself on me too. I suspected that all people build their forecasts for their futures from what they have learned, regardless of its source, and from what they believe and hope.

Dr. Zipp reacted differently. He thought I had received "a gift." I had received "hints of my destiny." I had been touched with "grace." He urged me not to discount it.

So I worked to synthesize my experience with what he had said and with Dr. Fleur's view. I knew I had almost died. (I had been coded twice, after all.) So perhaps what my consciousness had repressed from my experiences in surgery had been my spirit ACTUALLY LEAVING my body, because it thought the rational part of me would have been freaked out if I had remembered this. Arguing against this was a lengthy article in the *NYRB*, analyzing the literature of near-death experiences and, because of how culturally specific they were – Christians seeing Jesus, Muslims seeing Mohammed – concluding that all such visions, like I had initially thought, were hallucinations, derived from the observer's life experience.

I had an explanation for that too. I recalled a comic book story from my childhood, in which space explorers (all male) from Earth land on an unknown planet, which is populated entirely by gorgeous women, who wine, dine and otherwise entertain them. The story's SHOCK-ending is that the damsels are actually, by human standards, hideous monsters who, wanting to lure and "fatten-up" the men, whom they intend to devour, have exercised powers of mind-control, in order to appear desirable and not repellant. So perhaps the spirit world, so as not to come on too shocking, tailors itself to appear inviting to each of us – Christian, Muslim, me.

Anyway, the unassailable truth I took away was how much I wanted to live. Mind and, it seemed, body fought to keep life going. I imagine that occurred in those surgical theaters as well. I believe it helped that I could not convince myself there was a place I preferred to be.

If there is, I remain content to wait to discover it.

CODA (Adele)

In early 2013, Bob invited me to collaborate on what has become I Will
Keep You Alive. *He had already published in* Broad Street *several
beautiful and searing pieces that covered his attacks, surgeries and recoveries.
He hoped to create a book length work that might help others confronted by
what he'd experienced but had been unable to expand what he had sufficiently.
"You remember things I don't," he said. "Your insights are fascinating and your
phrasings unique. Let's do it together."*

*I had been struggling to settle into new writing, or revise old writings, but
my head was still spinning from the past two years. I didn't seem able to write
about them myself or to write something else. When each start ended unfinished,
I was disappointed. Taking care of Bob had occupied me. But now I could find
no desires of my own to carry forward. Like Bob, I wanted to feel "Terrific." We
both knew I had to move beyond the no-longer-necessary role of caretaker and
re-enter my life as a person, writer and wife. The feelings I'd had from taking
care of Bob had been golden, but as his recovery, physically and emotionally,
lapped my own, I remained stymied. The proposed collaboration became a locus
of hope, the invitation flattering and exciting. But the decision to join forces was
a gradual process.*

*Collaboration was not new for us. We had co-authored articles, and we
regularly helped each other by discussing current projects, reading drafts, and
offering suggestions. This had been a wonderful part of our relationship and,
when Bob had begun writing, after each heart attack and surgery, using my
mind to help him had helped keep me afloat. Our relationship seemed the green,
glowing edge of life, and the collaboration seemed a hopeful choice; but I could not
commit to it until I felt better than I did.*

It was not easy.

*In May, on a narrow, tree-lined path, I took a hurried step to avoid an on-
coming runner, slipped on loose pebbles and undergrowth, crashed into a tree
trunk, and tumbled to the ground. An x-ray at Alta Bates showed a vertical*

fracture, from my shoulder halfway down the humerus of my dominant arm. The orthopod put me in a sling. I could not raise my arm above shoulder-level. If sufficient bone growth did not occur, he would have to operate. Either way, I would never regain full ROM.

Bob took care of me. He helped me to the bathroom at night, helped me bathe, prepared our meals. He shampooed and straightened my hair. He bought me voice-recognition software for my computer, so I could write if I wanted. I would lay out tasks, and he would do them. "It's easy," he said he had come to recognize, "if you love the other person."

The pain medication, along with the anti-depressants already on board, loosened the grip of my obsessive thoughts and rituals. When I was well enough to exercise on the bike and treadmill at the club, I was so grateful! I let people help me dress, turn on the shower, open my shampoo bottle, and tie my shoes. I felt warmed by their attentiveness. As I figured out how to do things myself, I did them with more pleasure and less pressure. It wasn't a trip to Hawaii, but it felt like the vacation I needed, even if it pushed writing further away.

Bob's death-by-brownie became another problem.

I'd obtained my own prescription for medical marijuanaland, via a no-questions-asked clinic, which advertised in a local give-away weekly. I'd hoped to find a particular polymorphous perverse state I'd experienced one night in the mid-1960s, when my mind and body had sprung wide open, and, while scenes from Shakespeare had played in the flames of a fireplace, I'd achieved something bigger than a vaginal/clitoral orgasm – although I may have had that too. I had been wary of the baked goods Bob had brought back from the café and pleaded with him to use our own stash. Though I'd lost that tug-of-war, I'd only taken the recommended amount of our blackberry-flavored, dark chocolate bar.

As we waited for what we'd eaten to kick in, I snuggled close to Bob on the bed and ran my fingertips lightly over his body, something he normally loved, hoping he'd do the same to me. When he didn't make a move or sound, I felt like I'd lost him. When he pushed my hand away, I felt angry, abandoned – and scared by my reaction, which had been magnified by my own stoned state, and accompanied by the return of the feeling from when he'd been in his coma and I couldn't reach him, I ran to the bathroom to weep.

When I returned, I found Bob disoriented and terrified. He seemed to both see me and not. "Hallucinating," he said. "Scared."

I had difficulty dialing the house phone. I'd forgotten how it worked. I tried my cell and reached 911. When I heard the sirens. I clutched the house keys and walked in a slow, exaggerated, jerky fashion to the front door, holding onto the wall like a bug to keep from falling. I had difficulty getting the key into the lock and turning it. I felt like I was made of spare parts, hastily assembled. The handsome young policemen or firemen – I wasn't sure which – couldn't have been friendlier or calmer. They didn't seem to notice my mental state.

After checking Bob's vitals, they put me in charge of reminding him his heart was fine. I was to make sure he stayed hydrated, peed in a bottle, and stayed in bed until he stopped hallucinating. They suggested he sleep as much as he could while the drug wore off.

When the men-in-blue-or-red left, I felt abandoned by them too. I resented having to play nursemaid again. I grew enraged at having had our day-off spoiled and being back in the position of worried caretaker. But I did everything I'd been told.

The terrors of that afternoon lingered, my resultant helpless rage a further impediment to moving forward with the collaboration. I felt I had to become stronger, now that my extreme vulnerability had shown itself. I had to believe more deeply in both Bob's wellness and my own before choosing to relive the two years of heart trouble through writing. I couldn't imagine voluntarily exposing myself to those memories, which had been exacerbated by seeing Bob vulnerable and frightened again.

The relieving thought I'd had about possessing no magic had fallen apart under the pressure of my reaction. I was done with marijuana. It hadn't brought me the creative burst or sexual release I'd craved. In fact, my inhibitions redoubled.

I did learn something valuable though. It occurred to me that many people, confronted with an ill and dependent loved one, have to manage the helpless rage and anxiety I had felt. I had not understood the burden taking-care-of could impose on others, or the decisions these others in a similar situation might have to make, since they had been absent for me while Bob was truly sick. I now felt empathy for those whose psychological make-up opened them to different feelings and responses. I had been admired and applauded for all I had done for Bob, but, I realized, others should be no less applauded for recognizing what they couldn't do and seeking needed help elsewhere. What constituted love and led to survival was a complex and personal issue.

By October, my arm had healed sufficiently that I could type. My obsessive preoccupations were low enough that there was room for creative thinking. It was then I fully committed to the collaboration. I would add my own thoughts, feelings and recollections to Bob's existing pieces. At first we'd thought we'd alternate chapters, but the duet, four hands on each, became our preference. It was more intimate with our two voices intertwining.

I hoped this would help me transition into writing of my own. I also hoped this would help me master the experiences of the last two years. In the past, after I'd written a piece, the traumatic memory of the event or person upon whom it had been based could come and go without ripping me in two. I hoped for that sort of recovery and relief.

And I hoped the collaboration would enrich our present. I looked forward to discussing the material with Bob and working our way through any impasses the writing brought. But I soon found the flood of memories and thoughts swept me into a dark place, and I would have to hide from the book for days or weeks, while I rebuilt the ground on which I'd stood. I was sorry for the shadows my bailing out cast. Bob was disappointed that I wouldn't discuss what I'd written, but, once I was done, I had to let go completely. I didn't want to describe my day's work or think about what I had to do next. Every moment that I engaged with that portion of that past brought back the trauma full throttle. I shook as I re-read e-mails I had written. My fingers spasmed as I wrote about them. I could only go an hour or two before closing up.

Plus, Bob's approach to narrative and sequence drove me crazy. It took a *while for us to understand and appreciate how differently we processed time. I could write about each day I remembered in detail. Bob could write paragraphs that covered months and captured their essence. Appreciating each other's process and making the most of each helped me move onward. Each sentence that succeeded, each eventual paragraph and chapter, brought me more time in the present, with more hope and resilience I could make it to the conclusion. On the days my writing went well, I was happy. When Bob admired my offerings, I was ecstatic.*

So I kept going. I salvaged material from those trauma-triggering e-mails and a sporadically kept, nearly illegible, often incorrectly dated journal I had maintained. I found other usable pages in files I had established when I had thought I might write a book about those years myself. I didn't know if we would realize what we had set out to do, but I was hopeful.

When I was most stuck, I would ask Bob to talk it out. Even at 3 a.m., our exchanges deepened the trust between us and filled me with hope, warmth and the will to get back to work. It also helped me to have Bob's finished chapters to read and study. If I needed to fit and trim my excesses, I did. And it was good to hear Bob say the strength and clarity of the feelings I had expressed had influenced his writing too.

My portions that most sizzled for Bob were the accounts of the times he spent in surgery, under anesthesia, in his coma, closest to death. Reading my writing gave him whiffs of what was inside him. It helped him become more conscious of what he had been through and left him more fully invested in life.

In the spring of 2015, Bob joined Mended Hearts, a national organization which brought survivors of heart surgeries into hospital wards to answer questions and address the anxieties of those beginning the recovery process. "Vertical role models," is how the woman who interviewed Bob described participants. When she heard all he'd been through, she called him "A gold mine!"

Care-givers can also participate, but I didn't feel ready for that. But one morning I accompanied Bob to Sutter and waited in the Family Resource Center while he made his rounds. The FRC is a clean, well-appointed room, where people wait for doctors come with news of how operations had gone and when and where they will be able to see their loved ones. The FRC is where I had waited, stone still, with icy hands and feet, for news from surgeons. It was here, on whose computers, I'd checked tennis results or answered e-mails while Bob slept.

As I sat among the waiting families, I thought I might, someday, be able to speak with them about my similar times. Or maybe not. I realized my anxiety about doing so was accompanied by anger at Bob's wish to do this generous giving-back. Part of me wanted him to be like me and wall it off, so he didn't regularly bring home reminders of what we'd been through. I knew that was irrational, that, as close as we were, we were separate people. He had no problem with my not participating, and I'd learn to live with his decision – and my own.

Now I am much better for the struggle too. Even though I skipped Mended Hearts. Even though I hadn't been able to think about what we'd been through. Even though the writing of this book had to be done in stages of numbness and distance. I became able to confront the events we'd experienced after I got them on the page. Writing each chapter allowed me windows of time to open my eyes to what was there and make the most of it, feeling again what I'd felt throughout, that much gets reburied, unnamed, unused, because it is just too much.

I have proved strong enough to survive the high waves and undertows of our traumatic years by putting them into words. It has not obliterated my memories of those bad times, but I no longer live in the moment-by-moment fear of what I do or might recall. Just yesterday, I forgot to turn on my I-phone for hours after Bob had left the house, and, when I remembered, didn't expect to find bad news waiting. I willingly went back to work, editing the last page of my Coda, to cross the finish line before I went to sleep, eager to know what I would dream.

APPENDIX: MY LUNCH WITH "DR. FLEUR"

One afternoon in late April 2016, I sat down to lunch with Luisa Munoz del Romeral, M.D., PhD. Dr. Munoz received her degree from the Universidad de Estudil Valladolid in Spain and studied in France before coming to the United States on a post-doctoral fellowship. She is also Adele's and my "Dr. Fleur."

Dr. Munoz had read our manuscript while it was in progress. She told us she would be happy to answer any questions we had. She also said it would be fine to use her actual name, but the three of us had grown so fond of her alias, we retained it in the text.

She and I met at Le Bateau Ivre, a cottage-turned-restaurant on Telegraph Avenue, in North Berkeley. (Adele had begun a new writing project and did not want to revisit moments that might get in the way.)

The one significant change in my situation, since the manuscript's conclusion, was that, a few weeks before this lunch, Dr. Munoz had raised the possibility that I stop taking Effient. Most people stay on their blood thinner a year or two. I had been on mine five, except for a few months in 2014, when I had stopped, only to experience the "very nothing" incident, after which I had resumed it. If I stayed on Effient, Dr. Munoz had explained, I risked having a brain bleed. But if I came off, I risked an incident that would be "something."

When she had finished explaining the options, no one spoke. Then I'd said, "I'm inclined to go off the blood thinner." The idea of a brain bleed was frightening. But I had survived "incidents," so...

"That's my inclination too," Dr. Munoz had said.

"I don't think either of us would do well with a brain bleed," Adele said.

A stress-echo had showed my heart seemed strong enough to bear the risk of stopping the blood thinner. While part of my heart was dead, which we already knew, my vessels were free of blockage or narrowing. Dr. Munoz had printed out a copy of the "picture" so I could look at it if

I became "nervy." I'd pinned it to my bulletin board above my desk and pushed my Effient bottle to the back of the shelf.

Dr. Munoz ordered a warm spinach salad and I a Caesar salad with chicken. After a discussion of each other's wedding rings and the Warriors, for whom her husband has season tickets, we talked about the book. I have edited the transcript of this conversation, and Dr. Munoz has reviewed it for accuracy.

"I remember vividly the day I met you, and I don't know why. Maybe because we developed this relationship, and I ended up liking you guys so much. I remember you on the gurney in Alta Bates. I remember the position of the gurney. I know exactly which room you were in the ER. That I can draw a picture of, and I remember talking to you, and I remember thinking, 'Oh, he's really going to be a difficult bun to chew.' You were, like, very inquisitive and very, like, 'Why?' and 'Are you sure?' I remember how you told me that you were swimming. I remember vividly the swimming part. How you felt. How you got more tired. How you got out. And I didn't know what was going on, until you declared yourself, and I said, 'No, no, no. We're gonna take you to the CATH lab.' Remember that?"

I said my memory was that the ER doctor had resisted her sending me home and that she had called in a tech, in whom she had confidence, to re-test me.

"The ER never get anything right," she said. "For them, everything is red, or everything is black. There's no in-between. Frequently, we have sent people home, because we don't have risk factors. Because the ER data is not good data. In your particular case, you had zero risk factors. You were the picture of health. You were skinny. You exercised regularly. You didn't smoke. It was perfect. The drug, which is a marker to see if there's something there, was nothing significant. It was something the cardiologist says 'Negative,' the ER says 'Positive.' If the negative is .03, yours was .07. You didn't have chest pain. The EKG was completely normal. Then something changed on the monitor.

"So then we called another EKG, and that was abnormal. So then I thought, Maybe I need to take you to the CATH lab."

"The other day you said at first you were scared of us. Adele and I had a good laugh about that. What did you mean?"

"There is a type of patient that... Not 'scary'; but you know me, and I always want to be as helpful as possible to patients. And I try to explain to them what is going on, so they understand, and I try to get them to do the right thing. That's why I'm there, right? I don't want them not to do the right thing, and I want to be able to help them to understand, which I think I know better, because that's my job. But there are certain people... I mean, I respect if you said, 'I totally understand. I know my risk. I know my benefit, but I choose not to do it.' I would be sad, because I would say, 'You know, you might die.' 'I understand that I might die, but I prefer to die.'

"But there are others, that they're really inquisitive, and they want to show you that you might be wrong, not for the right reason, but because they might be afraid. This kind of patient is difficult to deal with. And I thought that Adele was going to be one of them, because she was going to be so afraid that it was going to be difficult for me to get to her heart and try to help you guys. That was my only hesitation. I thought, 'Oh my God, it's going to be difficult, and at the end of the day, they're going to piss me off, and I'm not going to have the patience to do the good thing for them.'"

"Was that something you thought from the beginning?"

"No, that was later. I remember you well on the ER, but, the first day, I don't have a clear recollection of Adele. She was there, but I didn't perceive how scared she was. I didn't perceive how important she was in the whole picture and what was her power. I was more afraid of you. But I wanted you to understand that something needed to be done. You were very inquisitive about 'Why?' and 'Are you sure' and 'What're you going to do?' and 'What is that going to do to me?' And then you put that face." She paused. "That face that you put now."

We both laughed.

"Like 'Are you sure that you know what you're doing?' Like 'I'm a lawyer.' And I was, I don't care that you're a lawyer. I want to do the right thing, because I want to save your life, dude! I'm not American. I don't care about sued. And Adele at that time was not on my radar as she was afterwards."

"One of the problems for Adele," I said, "was that she didn't know what was going on inside of me, so she would think, in some situations, that I was in more trouble than I really was. Plus she tends to go on the Internet and read things that raise questions and I don't. I just believe whatever my doctor says."

Dr. Munoz said, "I learned that about her later, when I would have to confront you with some news, and she would be the one telling me, 'Why?' and 'Are you sure that's the right thing to do?' 'What is going to happen?' 'What if it doesn't work?' All this questions will come from her, not from you. And that is difficult when you want to have a good outcome that you know the data too, so you're trying to be the positive thinking person in the group but without hiding the truth."

I did not say that Adele and I would go over questions we might ask beforehand. I said, "That seemed to be a key to your approach, to encourage the patient to think positively; and for us it worked very well."

"You guys wrote something that touched my heart so profoundly, about when you were at Summit, after the second heart attack. Little by little, you knew you were getting better, but still we had the valve business. We were over one major problem but facing the other. It was a couple of days before you were discharged home. You were really afraid, and she was even more afraid of how life was going to be for you, and how you were going to deal with it. It was a chapter that you wrote about the tree that was behind your room, So she said, both of you said that 'Dr. Fleur will come and make rounds and we will wait for her like the flowers turn to the sun'; and I thought that was such an absolutely fantastic and beautiful. I said, 'Nobody has ever said anything like this from me.' That was really nice.

"It's true."

"But at that time, I had that connection already. I knew that I could talk to her, and she was going to be frightened, but I could make her feel better or feel a little of my hope. I was trying to give to her, like it is going to be difficult, but it will be light at the end of the tunnel. So then I think things start getting better for her."

"Remember in the ER, when you asked me about vitamins and supplements. and you told me...

"'Stop them all!' She laughed. "This is part of the problem when you work in Berkeley, right. Because there is people that believe that these supplements will do much better for them than doing the right thing. In general, it's been proven that, you open up the capsules and do the DNA, and there is nothing in them. But sometimes they put something, which you don't know what it is, that can really, really harm people. I've seen people that've been taking some herb from the Hindu Kush that will make you lose weight and get really sick, so that's why I said, 'You have no risk factors. You've been doing all your life the right things, and look what happens.' I don't want you to put anything in your body that I can not control, because I don't know what that is. I'm super against it."

"You had said you noticed changes in my personality, and Adele wanted me to ask what kind and when they happened."

"Maybe it was not like you changed. Maybe it is that I come to know you better. But I saw, after the first heart attack, I saw that confrontation with what happened with you being kind of weird for somebody who has done always the right thing. You went back to work. You did rehab. You enjoyed rehab, and then all your stents cut off. They had to rescue you, take you to Summit. You were incubated. You went through that. And when you start coming back, I start noticing that you were, like, 'What's going on?' Like 'I'm back here, and what's gonna keep going on?' And the first light in your eyes was when you saw that you were going to leave the hospital. That you were able to go back home. But at the same time, you had that big question mark, like, 'What kind of life am I gonna have?'

157

"Then, when you come to the office, I could perceive, like a newborn, you learned again how to enjoy the beauty of being able to go to the café and read a book; and I remember you coming, 'And today I walked all the way to...' Whatever. "And 'Today I went up stairs and I didn't feel bad.' I heard that change in your mind. Like everybody else you had it for granted. Until you were sick, you didn't know the beauty of being able to walk around the block; and I have seen you discovering little things and being amazed by how great life can be, like, if you're able to have Caesar salad with chickens. All these things, I thought, were making you more human, like a nicer person; and at the same time, because Adele was your nurse, it was making her also to grow as a person. I mean, I think she grew up taller and stronger, because I think she found a way to show you her love in a different way, like nursing you, right? And it was something that she hadn't done before."

"She learned she was capable of doing that."

"And that made her not to be afraid. She did a great job. She did an *amazing* job! Better than any nurse, right. All this, from outside, I was seeing it, happening between. It made me happy."

After I had ordered an espresso and Dr. Munoz a non-fat cappuccino, I asked about the device she had been excited by at the conference she'd attended in 2011.

"At that time, I was thinking you might not make it. The heart might not get better. You might not be able to have a normal life. So the options are transplant, which is, like, the best option of the heart. But that comes with a huge price, because you get a new heart, but then you might find you have a new cancer, because the medications that reduce for rejection will kill your good cells that will protect you from cancer; and frequently, ten years after, people develop lymphoma. But it's still the best option."

I calculated, Okay, ten years, I'll be eighty-four. That's not necessarily a deal-killer.

She went on, "The other is a machine that pulls the blood out of the heart, like a pump, and returns the blood back to the heart. You put it inside the body, but, still, you have a cable outside, connected to the batteries, and is cumbersome; but it keeps you alive and having an almost normal life. So I was trying to say, if you don't make it, we going to give you a heart; and if things got really really sour, we can use one of these pumps to breach you until transplant. You were qualified for a transplant, because you were healthy, young, smart; but you don't know when you're going to get it, and you have to keep a patient alive. So we develop these things; now they are smaller, and, in three years, it will be fully implanted, and the patient will not be connected to any batteries. It will be like a pacemaker.

"I was trying to say, 'Don't worry. I will do anything that I have to do to keep you alive.' Whether I have to put you on a machine. Whether I have to breach you to transplant. I will keep you alive, I promise, until I can get a heart."

I will keep you alive. I promise. The words touched something deep inside me. "I wonder why there are so many books written by people who survive cancer, but, aside from Dick Cheney, not many from survivors of heart troubles. Maybe it was big news he had one."

She laughed. "I think the perception is that cancer is something from outside, an invader, an enemy fighting against your body. But your heart is part of you. There is nothing from outside. There is nothing you can fight against. You want your heart to start working, like 'C'mon buddy, get it together. You have to work. You have to heal.' You can not be mad at your heart. You can be mad at a cancer, because it's a tumor. It's invading you. It's a different concept."

I read my next question. "Does your practice always send people to cardio-rehab? When I see people in Mended Hearts, I'm never sure whether to mention it or not."

"One hundred percent. We are huge on rehab, and there is tons of data, and it has been shown to be so good. First, it gives the confidence. Second... With other injuries, everybody rehabs it, and everybody understand that is a good thing. Why would you not rehab your heart? Is the same."

"Do some doctors not…"

"Oh, tons of them. They don't care. A ton of cardiologists, it's like 'Okay. Done. That's it. Next. Heal. Take your pills.' They don't understand you have to be really preventive, and you have to work really hard on, 'So this gentleman had a heart attack. Why?' 'You had a heart attack. We fix it.' That is not important. The important is 'Why did he have a heart attack? How can I prevent that he has another one?' That is, to me, my really important approach to a patient. Is not 'Okay, I put a stent; here, take your pills. That's it.' Is amazing a lot of doctors are like that. I know, because I see some of their patients for their follow up. I look at where they are. Oh my God! How can they be on this med? 'Did such and such talk to you about what you weigh?' 'No. You're the only one who mention the weight.' How can they not mention the weight? 'You're diabetic, dude. You're going to have another heart attack. Did they tell you that you had the first one because of the weight?' 'No.' They don't want confrontation. They don't care. It's in and out. It's how to measure productivity at the end of the year. How many patients you saw. There's no productivity based on how good your job was done."

"When we were talking about my going off the Effient, and you explained the risks and didn't jump in with your recommendation, it made me think about the tremendous weight people in your profession carry around. It's not just me. It's the next patient, and the next patient, and the next patient. You have life and death decisions to make with everyone. With me, when I was a lawyer, it was just, 'How much money will I get someone?'"

"And some time, you know, you say, 'What if I'm not right? What if I kill him?' You live with that all your life. I'm normally very studious, and I always have the data, right, because that can force me so I know. I say 'Okay. These are the choices.' You go from data. 'Seventy percent is A. Thirty percent is B. Da da da. I think in your case it should be done because of that.'

"But in your particular case, there's no data. You plugged all your stents on Plavix. We didn't find any specific problem with your

160

coagulation that we could tap into it. We put you on Effient; you did well. We stop Effient, and there was that thing, which we never know what it was. George (Galloway) got scared, because I went to the CATH lab immediately, and I said, 'Show me.' And it was wishy-washy. If it was somebody else, not you, with your history, we would maybe proceed in a different way. So the reaction was... You're back on Effient.

"But then we went over that hump, and I start thinking, 'What if I make him bleed from the head?' I mean, Who's crazy? So then... They did a study after that, on two years, but not on five. So I started looking in the two years. And they developed a risk score; so now, the patient you keep on for two years, you do the risk score and say, 'Okay, what are the chances that he's gonna bleed, or what are the chances he's gonna have a heart attack?' Then based on that, I make my decisions. But you were out of the charts. You did not have any reason for happening what happened. You were not diabetic, not hypertensive. You had no renal... You were young. So after five years, I said, 'What am I treating?' Am I treating our fears?' That is not the right thing to do. Because for treating our fears, I might make you bleed from the brain. So that's when I said, 'We've got to get over this?' But I wanted you to be in the boat with me, and Adele too."

I took this in.

"I wanted you to be involved, because I thought that you would be less anxious if you were part of the decision making. You will have my inclination for stopping, but knowing how anxious that was going to make, I was going to give to you part of it. Not because I wanted to share the responsibility, but because I wanted you to be happy with it."

"I have pretty good defenses," I said.

Dr. Munoz laughed.

I brought up Dr. Volpe's suspicion that my bleeding was my fault.

"The big fear of a surgeon," she said, "is blood. I sent you to that hospital, because I wanted to be sure that we had the back-up of a pump if anything would happen to you. And I made it myself clear, when I talked to him, 'Hey, what I want is your back-up.' He's a good surgeon.

But I'm just trying to make him, 'I am not sending you my patient because you're such a good surgeon. I'm sending you my patient because, here, I choose Dr. Doumajian to do the surgery, but I'm afraid that the heart might not make it without the pump, and, right now, we don't have anything, and it will be too risky to go over the bridge for the heart pump. So for that reason I'm sending him to you."

"He wrote that he lifted out my heart. Is that true? They lift it out. What do they do with it?" I laughed, this time nervously.

"They put it in the hands."

"Is it disconnected from everything?"

"No, they continue to connect it. They don't cut the main vessels. But they lift it to approach the mitral valve. Yeah, they have the heart in the hands. Your heart is totally stopped with a solution with potassium, and you do everything with the heart stopped. They bypass your blood from your main arteries, and they get all the blood that is going to the heart to a machine that pumps it back, in and out, in and out, in and out. Then when you sure that the sutures are competent and is not a hole in there, you stop the pump. You get the heartbeat, and then you look and see if it's leaking all over. If there's a major leak, you stop the heart again, and go back on the pump; and then you, like, 'Okay, now I don't have any blood.' So when they're happy, they say, 'That's it.' They close.

"With surgeons, you want somebody who know how to do that particular surgery better than anyone else. You don't care whether they are morons. You want good hands. That's all. That's what I want from a surgeon. I *will* take care of a patient. I *know* when the surgery has to be done. I don't want them dictating to me. I want them to operate. Do it in the minimum time. Perfect stitches. Do it the way it should be. Check back, and then don't touch it. I don't want them to be fancy. If they are smart, you know, better; but it's not required.

"I know that is a very weird approach, but it's something that you do with your hands. You want ability. You want dexterity. The surgeon has to be neat. Has to be very Type A and everything to be right there, where it should be. That is, what is to me, a good surgeon. I think surgery continues being, how can I say it... Surgery is for the part of medicine that won't resolve. We can not cure with the surgery. So I think with time we become better and better, surgery is going to go down and down. Surgery is when we don't know what else to do, we cut; right? Think about that. We doctors try to cure; we try to restore the organ. Surgeons cut it up."

While I absorbed that, I showed Dr. Munoz my after-lunch vitamins. Two Gummy Vites and one gold D.

"Those are good," she said. "Take them."

There was one last thing I wanted to ask. "Why did you call us your favorite couple?"

"Because is the truth. You are my favorite couple. By now you know I say what I think, right, and I have lots of couples that I care for a long long time. Maybe they don't need me as much, but I never felt the contact so close as I did with you and Adele.

I sipped my espresso.

"You guys are different, both, and different from each other. Adele has an enormous sensibility. She's super smart. The way she behaves is different. And you too. From day one, I knew you were different. I remember when you say, 'We celebrate Thanksgiving with pasta and clam sauce.' I don't know. I'm always... 'This is bright and different and interesting.' Sometimes one part of the couple is like that, but the other is... More regular.

"Then I heard the story of how you got together, and I thought it was super interesting, and I was really attracted to your personalities, and I liked to be there for you, and you... I don't know. How do you love someone? Maybe it is biological. Maybe it's genetic. Maybe it's because something resonates to you. And then we did so many things together, right. That made me feel close to you."

"We feel that way about you too. You know, it's just a different relationship from when you see a doctor, like once a year and they check whatever they're supposed to check, and then you go away. But, with you, it was like, 'My life is in your hands.'" I shook my head, as I had often come to do in the past five years, at the wonder of it all.

"Another thing that attracted me to you guys, how different personalities you both were; and yet I saw how the love for each other grew. That I saw. That was so precious to witness. The communication that you guys have is so amazing and so difficult to find in people. That sort of a dependence on each other. Maybe it was there all the time, but I saw it developing in front of my eyes, and I loved that. I thought it was so tender and so nice. That as a human being made me feel better about us as people."

It had been two hours. Dr. Munoz had parked at CVS and feared being towed. I had my "Disabled" placard and need not hurry. It was such a unique and wonderful relationship, I thought, custom-tailored without the angles and edges that complicate things with family and friends. She had once said to us that, on rough days, my case reminded her why she went into her business. For us, the entire experience hovered within a pocket of consciousness that words can touch but not contain.

How do you come to love somebody? Dr. Munoz had said. Our book was about that too.

ACKNOWLEDGMENT (Adele)

I offer thanks from the bottom of my heart to the doctors who helped save Bob's life and to the nurses who tended and watched over him with skill and care while he healed. I learned much from each of you. And thanks to our "Saint," Dr. Fleur, the third voice of this book, who gave her intelligent attention, her positivity and love, to all matters of mind and body throughout. It made all the difference.

I thank the friends and family who lived through the I Will Keep You Alive *years with us, and who each cared and helped in key ways.*

Bob and I have made many journeys together since we first met, but that described by I Will Keep You Alive *, with all its moments, anguished and sweet, has had the most profound effect on our relationship. "In sickness and in health," once just words… If there was ever any doubt, there is none now. We are in this together. We have, as we still say to each other each night before sleep, been lucky, blessed and loved.*

ACKNOWLEDGMENT (Bob)

Me too.

We also thank Milo George, our "production guy" for formatting, proofreading, copyediting and generally performing as a "fixer" at a level that made Michael Cohen look like, if you'll excuse the obscure *MAD* comic reference, Frank N. Stein's assistant Bumble; Marc Arsenault, who hung with us through my numerous, sometimes repeated "What-is-going-on?" grade-school level questions, while hooking us up with a major distributor; Francois Vigneault, whose stunning cover swatted Adele's and my ideas back into the slush pile and convinced us we should stick to words; Mary Bisbee-Beek, our sterling publicist, without whose efforts you probably would never have heard of this book, let alone picked it up and read this far; and Dan Rottenberg, who, as editor of *The Broad Street Review*, ran my initial pieces over the complaints of readers more comfortable with reviews of plays and art exhibits than this old guy with heart problems.

ABOUT THE AUTHORS

Adele Levin is a retired DMH (Doctor of Mental Health). Her short stories have appeared, among other places, in *Chiron Review*, *The Sun*, *Yellow Silk* and *Sex in San Francisco*.

Bob Levin is a retired attorney (workers' compensation). His books include *The Best Ride to New York*, *The Pirates and the Mouse*, *Cheesesteak* and *The Schiz*.

The Levins have lived in Berkeley for over 50 years.